SENIOR MISSIONS

WHAT TO EXPECT AND HOW TO PREPARE

SENIOR
MISSIONS

What to Expect
and How to Prepare

Marnae B. Wilson

CFI

AN IMPRINT OF CEDAR FORT, INC.

SPRINGVILLE, UTAH

Cover photo courtesy of Dave and Kymm Story.

ISBN 13: 978-1-4621-2011-6

Published by CFI, an imprint of Cedar Fort, Inc., 2373 W. 700 S., Springville, UT 84663
Distributed by Cedar Fort, Inc., www.cedarfort.com

LIBRARY OF CONGRESS CATALOGING-IN-PUBLICATION DATA

Names: Wilson, Marnae B., author.
Title: Senior missions : what to expect and how to prepare / Marnae B. Wilson.
Description: Springville, UT : CFI, an imprint of Cedar Fort, Inc., [2017] |
    Includes bibliographical references and index.
Identifiers: LCCN 2016055847 (print) | LCCN 2017001138 (ebook) | ISBN
    9781462120116 (pbk. : alk. paper) | ISBN 9781462127702
Subjects: LCSH: Mormon missionaries--Training of. | Older people in
    missionary work--Church of Jesus Christ of Latter-day Saints. | Married
    people in missionary work--Church of Jesus Christ of Latter-day Saints. |
    Church of Jesus Christ of Latter-day Saints--Missions.
Classification: LCC BX8661 .W537 2017 (print) | LCC BX8661 (ebook) | DDC
    266/.893320846--dc23
LC record available at https://lccn.loc.gov/2016055847

Cover design by Kinsey Beckett
Cover design © 2017 by Cedar Fort, Inc.
Edited and typeset by Chelsea Holdaway

Printed in the United States of America

10 9 8 7 6 5 4 3 2 1

Printed on acid-free paper

This book is dedicated to all the people, including senior missionary couples, who bring their small offerings of loaves and fishes to the Savior's table, where He magnifies those offerings into a feast that feeds His children throughout the world.

Contents

Introduction

A LITTLE HELP FROM A FRIEND

So you're thinking about going on a mission. Wonderful! There are few periods in your life when you can feel like all of your time and talent is being used to serve our Heavenly Father and build His kingdom. One of those times is while you are having and raising children, and another is while you are serving a mission. In fact, serving a mission is a lot like having a baby. It is full of wonderful surprises and amazing challenges. It stretches you in ways you'd never have guessed, and it makes you into a new and better person. You and your children and your children's children will be eternally blessed because you made the choice to serve.

This book was written to be your big sister—a sister who has already gone on a senior mission and can give you useful advice. It's not supposed to be "everything there is to know about missions." It's supposed to be a resource for you that has practical answers to practical questions.

Sometimes you might be afraid to go on a mission because you don't know what to expect or how to handle all the new adventures a mission holds. I am here to help! Challenges can be resolved and fears can be calmed with a little help from a fellow senior sister.

Just as an experienced mother can help you learn how to survive pregnancy, nurse a baby, or calm a colicky child, I can help you fill out your colicky mission application papers, choose what clothes to take, deal with language and cultural challenges, and strengthen your marriage in stressful times.

Your mission will be one of the greatest experiences of your life, and if you have a little help from a friend, it can also be fun, exciting, and amazingly edifying. Just as having and raising a baby is not problem-free, neither is a mission, but with a little help, you can love the ride and grow from your problems instead of just enduring them.

So let's begin this adventure together! There are so many simple things you can do to enhance your mission experience. You just need to know where to start.

Missions and Me

Since I had always planned to serve a mission, as soon as I graduated from BYU in 1970, I submitted my application papers. I was called to serve in the Brazil Central Mission and entered the Language Training Mission, which preceded the current Provo Missionary Training Center, before I had actually turned twenty-one (which was the required age for sister missionaries at the time).

While in Brazil, I was called to be the zone leader over a zone of sister missionaries. As I served, I learned a great deal about myself and about missionary realities from dedicated and talented sister missionaries.

It was when I was sixty that the bishop called me and my husband, Bruce, in to visit with him. We expected to be asked to help in the nursery or to be given another calling, but instead, the bishop held up the most recent senior missionary bulletin and said, "When I received this bulletin in the mail, it seemed to have your names written on it."

We replied that we intended to serve a mission, but we were thinking of later, after we had retired and paid off our home. He said that his impression was that we should consider serving right away, and he asked us to go home and pray about it.

In shock, we began to consider the ramifications of quitting our jobs and leaving our home and family. But the more we discussed the possibility, the more we felt like it was something we should do. So we called the bishop and began the application process.

A few months later, we received our call to serve as the office mission couple for the Portugal Porto Mission. We loved serving in the office and interacting with all the missionaries. We loved helping the missionaries fix their broken plumbing and aching hearts. We loved working with our dear mission president and his wife. And we loved traveling all over northern Portugal.

But out of the blue, we received notice that our mission was being combined with the Portugal Lisbon Mission. Since they already had a mission couple, we were asked to serve as Member and Leader Support (MLS) missionaries on the southern coast of Portugal.

This was before the Church provided apartments for senior couples, so we packed up our old apartment and moved to Faro, Portugal, where we found a wonderful, inexpensive apartment in the middle of a citrus orchard.

Oh, the adventures we had in Faro. As we searched to find unknown members whose names were on the branch rolls, we discovered old town Faro and enjoyed the beauties of the Portuguese Riviera. We gasped as our little car squeezed around blind corners on narrow, cobblestone streets. We laughed with the members as we taught dance classes. We cried when we had to leave the young men we had helped baptize. What sweet memories!

However, while serving this mission, I was surprised to see some couple missionaries struggling in ways they hadn't anticipated. Some struggled with health problems. Some felt left out and isolated when they could not speak the language their spouse had learned on a prior mission. Some found that the favorite recipes they brought would not work with the ingredients available in their mission country. After shedding many sympathetic tears with these missionaries, I realized that many of their stresses and struggles could have been avoided if they had had a better idea of what to expect and how to prepare for their mission experience.

Only a few months after we had returned home from Portugal, we discovered that the Church needed attorneys to serve in area offices around the world. So we spoke with the Church's legal department, submitted our papers, and prepared to serve in the Brazil Area office. However, after we waited almost nine months for Brazilian visas, the legal office asked us to serve in the Africa Southeast Area office.

This mission was almost completely served in the area office in Johannesburg, South Africa. Bruce spent his days solving legal problems, and I had the amazing opportunity to work on the area website, collecting, editing, and publishing stories of the faithful African Saints. We also got to serve in a local ward supporting the young single adults.

We have rarely had the opportunity to use our talents in such meaningful ways. We stretched, we learned, we grew, and we knew that we were building the Lord's kingdom in ways we had never anticipated.

Will we serve another mission? We don't know. If the Lord calls again, we'll go where He wants us to go.

A Look Inside the Book

This book walks you through the process of going on a senior couple mission, starting with deciding to serve, moving through the application process, giving support for the major decisions you'll have to make, and exploring the initial adjustments you'll encounter as you begin to serve.

Chapter 1, "Should I Go?," discusses the benefits of serving a mission, including what Church leaders have said and what opportunities are available for senior missionaries.

Chapter 2, "I'm Not Ready!," provides suggestions for preparing spiritually, financially, physically, and emotionally. We also share ideas for strengthening your marriage and improving your skills.

Chapter 3, "On Your Mark, Get Set, Apply!," gives step-by-step instructions on processing your mission application, including detailed information on what is included in the application process and what medical clearances are required.

Chapter 4, "Your Call Is Here—Now What?," discusses information about the specifics of your mission and how to get answers to your questions.

Chapter 5, "Money Matters," gives you options and suggestions for dealing with your home, your taxes, and your bank while you're away.

Chapter 6, "Health Concerns," introduces discussions about health limitations, insurance, medical tests, medications, and immunizations.

Chapter 7, "Clothing and Appearance," provides detailed information on clothing selection, accessories, cosmetics, and hair issues.

Chapter 8, "All Things Electrical and Electronic," gives suggestions for phones, computers, e-books, electrical appliances, adaptors, DVDs, and music you can bring with you on your mission.

Chapter 9, "A Whole Mission in Two Suitcases—Are You Kidding?," shares ideas for effective and efficient packing.

Chapter 10, "Getting There," suggests ways to make travelling to your mission more comfortable.

Chapter 11, "The Missionary Training Center," provides all the details you'll want to know about the Missionary Training Center, including getting there, housing, expenses, and classes.

Chapter 12, "Mission Realities," explains what to expect when you first arrive in your mission and what adjustments you'll encounter.

Chapter 13, "Culture Shock," addresses unexpected differences you'll notice in your new setting, such as traffic, laws, food, language, and schedules.

Chapter 14, "Marriage Adjustments," suggests ways to keep your marriage healthy while serving together.

Chapter 15, "Family Concerns," provides encouragement as you ponder leaving your children, grandchildren, and aging parents.

Chapter 16, "Precious Memories," shares a few of my favorite memories that made our missions worth every sacrifice.

At the end of the book, Appendix A lists online resources you'll use over and over, Appendix B lists countries and their electrical standards, and Appendix C provides illustrations of the different types of electrical outlets used throughout the world.

Let's get started!

Chapter 1

SHOULD I GO?

In 2012, President Monson announced the new age requirements for junior missionaries. Young people by the thousands began applying to serve missions, and some of us who had been mission office couples thought, "Wow! We are going to need tons of senior couples to take care of all these missionaries! Who is going to process their papers? Who is going to find them apartments? Who is going to send them mission information? Who is going to help the mission presidents survive?"

We senior office couples weren't the only ones who were worried about the pending changes. Church leaders knew this change would make the need for couple missionaries even greater. Years before the age change was announced, Church leaders began asking senior members to prepare for missions.

In 2010, President Monson pleaded, "We need many, many more senior couples. . . . Make yourselves available to leave home and give full-time missionary service. There are few times in your lives when you will enjoy the sweet spirit and satisfaction that come from giving full-time service together in the work of the Master."[1]

And then, just a year later in 2011, Elder Holland exclaimed, "We need thousands of more couples serving in the missions of the Church. Every mission president pleads for them. Everywhere they serve, our couples bring a maturity to the work that no number of nineteen-year-olds, however good they are, can provide."[2]

The Church leaders knew how difficult it would be for older couples, who have physical and financial limitations, to leave their homes and families. But they also knew that the sacrifice would yield unbelievable blessings for the couples and their families.

As Elder David B. Haight said,

> Serving a mission gives retired people a chance to use their talents and gifts again. They discover that they are truly needed, and as a consequence they find a powerful new sense of direction in life. They joyfully lose themselves in new experiences and opportunities for growth. The reward for those who serve is often renewed health and energy. When they go home, they are filled with the rich spirit of missionary work and a great love for the people they have served.[3]

Elder Vaughn J. Featherstone added,

> Let our missionary ranks swell to tens of thousands of couples. This is one of the great solutions to the evil in our generation. Our generation can and will make a difference in this great world. Let us all examine our hearts and prove to the Lord that we "will go and do the things which the Lord hath commanded." . . . Oh, my dearly beloved mature couples, let's rise up as a generation and do magnificent and wonderful things. . . . Collectively, in going into the mission field by the thousands and thousands, we as couples can lay one more great spiritual contribution on the altar of God.[4]

One senior sister remembers reading Moroni's letter to Pahoran in Alma 60:5–8, in which he exclaimed in frustration,

> It might have otherwise been if ye had rendered unto our armies sufficient strength and succor. Yea, great has been your neglect towards us.
>
> And now behold, we desire to know the cause of this exceedingly great neglect; yea, we desire to know the cause of your thoughtless state.
>
> Can you think to sit upon your thrones in a state of thoughtless stupor, while your enemies are spreading the work of death around you?
>
> Yea, even they who have looked up to you for protection, yea, have placed you in a situation that ye might have succored them, yea, ye might have sent armies unto them, to have strengthened them, and have saved thousands of them from falling by the sword.

This sister was amazed at how much this reprimand applied to senior couples who refuse to leave the comfort of their homes, refusing to succor missionaries, members, investigators, and nonmembers.

As she continued reading verse 11, she felt even more chastised: "Behold, could ye suppose that ye could sit upon your thrones, and because of the exceeding goodness of God ye could do nothing and he would deliver you? Behold, if ye have supposed this ye have supposed in vain."

She shared her insights with her husband, and within a short time, they began looking at the current Senior Missionary Opportunities Bulletin[5] and figuring out ways to fit a mission into their lives

The decision to serve a mission should not be taken lightly.

As Elder Robert D. Hale instructs, "Counsel with your extended family and your bishop or branch president. As the

Lord's servants understand your temporal situation, you will be able to receive the eternal blessing of full-time missionary service."[6]

Many couples think, "Of course we're going to serve a mission—in about five years. First we need to get our basement finished." Or "We want to wait until our grandkids are baptized." Or "We just want to travel a bit first."

Unfortunately, one excuse leads to another, and before they know it, to quote Helaman 13:38, "Ye have procrastinated the day of your [mission] until it is everlastingly too late."

Don't let your neighbors, your children, or your friends decide if and when you should serve a mission.

You, your spouse, and your Heavenly Father need to make those decisions. There will always be reasons not to go. But there will also be good reasons to serve. Take your concerns to the Lord, and He will direct your paths (see Proverbs 3:6).

As Elder David B. Haight said: "There is often a real fear in [couples'] minds—fear of not being able to measure up, of being embarrassed, of climbing stairs, of slipping on the ice, of many other things. But there really isn't much to be afraid of, because assignments are made by people who understand the situation. . . . These priesthood leaders know that married couples fill a void that no one else can fill. And they know many great ways couple missionaries can serve and how they can be productive."[7]

Don't worry too much about your limitations. Because of the great variety of missionary opportunities, there is certainly a place for you. Before you apply, you may need to take some time to organize your finances, figure out how to manage your home, counsel with your families, and stabilize some of your health problems, but you can serve a mission.

There are missions that can be done from your own home, using your personal computer. There are missions that can be served in your own stake. There are missions that can be served in your local family history center. There is a huge variety of ways you can help build God's kingdom here on earth. You just have to open your heart and mind and figure out how to make it happen.

So put down that remote and come out of hibernation. Get off your thrones and get busy. There are people all over the world who are dying spiritually, and you might have succored them and saved thousands of them from falling by the wayside. All it takes is a first step forward.

Summary

- The Church needs thousands and thousands of senior missionary couples.
- There are many varied ways to serve a mission.
- Don't procrastinate the day of your mission.
- Counsel with the Lord about your mission plans.

Notes

1. Thomas S. Monson, "As We Meet Together Again," *Ensign*, November 2010.
2. Jeffrey R. Holland, "We Are All Enlisted," *Ensign*, November 2011.
3. David B. Haight, "Couple Missionaries—'A Wonderful Resource,'" *Ensign*, February 1996.
4. Vaughn J. Featherstone, "Couple Missionaries: 'Too Wonderful for Me,'" *Ensign*, September 1998.
5. www.lds.org/bc/content/ldsorg/callings/missionary/senior -missionary/senior-missionary-opportunities.pdf?lang=eng.
6. Robert D. Hales, "Couple Missionaries: Blessings from Sacrifice and Service," *Ensign*, May 2005.
7. Haight, "Couple Missionaries—'A Wonderful Resource.'"

Chapter 2

I'M NOT READY!

When you think of serving a mission, you may panic. "I'm just not ready!" "I haven't been exercising regularly—actually, not at all." "My spouse has diabetes." "I never learned to use a computer." "I've only read the Book of Mormon once, and the Old Testament—are you kidding?" You may think there is no way to make up for years and years of being more or less slothful in this or that. Now the day of reckoning is at hand, and you wonder how you can make up for lost time.

You can take comfort from Elder Robert D. Hales: "Your life is your preparation. You have valuable experience. You have raised a family and served in the Church. Just go and be yourselves. The Lord has promised that angels will go before you (see D&C 103:19–20)."[1]

There are, however, several things you can do to prepare for your mission *long before* you talk to the bishop and begin filling out your application. If you don't do some long-term preparation, you're going to get your papers and then end up waiting for a year to get ready, doing things like trying to recover from a necessary operation or trying to sell your house.

Spiritual Preparation

Remember when you were in school and used to read a whole unit in one night so you could pass the test the next day? Well, that doesn't really work very well with spiritual preparation. And honestly, you can't just assume your spouse will know all the answers when gospel questions come up.

Some of the most valuable missionary work you will do is sister to sister and brother to brother. When you make comments in a little branch's Relief Society meeting, you are teaching the gospel. When you comfort a suffering member or investigator, you are sharing your testimony. Being spiritually prepared is using the gospel in your life to solve problems and overcome weaknesses. Yes, it's great to know just where Lehi said, "For it must needs be, that there is an opposition in all things," and yes, it really was Lehi who said that (2 Nephi 2:11). But it is much more valuable to stay faithful when you encounter opposition in your own life, and understand that opposition is a blessing. Then you can share your knowledge and testimony with people who need your spiritual strength.

Nevertheless, it's pretty much essential to be studying the scriptures regularly. If you haven't been doing that, you may want to start. You don't have to do a marathon. In fact, reading a massive number of pages in one sitting will likely be counterproductive. Half your brain will be reading along happily while the other half will be planning what to fix for dinner. That's why the prophets counsel us to study the scriptures regularly and ponder them. Spirituality is gained bit by bit. Ask the five foolish virgins (see Matthew 25:1–13) just how well a crash course in righteousness worked out for them.

You may want to choose one book of the standard works to study and read it through. If you choose to take that approach for your studies, it might be helpful to get the seminary or institute manual that accompanies whichever volume of scripture you chose and read it as you go. Or you may decide to study one particular concept of the gospel, such as faith or humility. If that is the approach you decide to take, the Bible Dictionary and the Topical Guide will be your best friends and you will enjoy yourself thoroughly as you go on footnote scavenger hunts.

Pray about what to focus on and which approach will work best for you, and then schedule a regular time to study. If you think you can just pick up the scriptures when you get a free moment, you're kidding yourself, and you know it. Set a regular time to study and stick to it. One sister decided she wouldn't eat until she had read her scriptures. Sometimes she got pretty hungry, but she did get her scriptures read. Of course, she didn't have to be at work at 8 a.m. Figure out what will work for you and then try harder than you did last time. After all, you have a really good reason to take this gospel study thing seriously now.

Right up there with studying the scriptures is reading and studying *Preach My Gospel*. You may think this book mostly teaches how to knock on doors effectively and how to function with a companion, and there is some of that. However, almost all of the book is about the basic principles of the gospel and how they work in people's lives. The book is easy to read and easy to understand. It's well organized by topic, and it is full of scripture references that you can look up as you study. If you're worried about being knowledgeable enough about the gospel, this book is for you.

Now this next suggestion may make you hesitate a bit, but really, if you could study *Preach My Gospel* together with your spouse, you would find it a very edifying experience. Realistically, not too many of us actually study the gospel with our spouses. We may have daily scripture study together, but we don't do much talking about what we read. If you use *Preach My Gospel* or an institute manual as the foundation for your daily study together and actually talk about what the books teach, you and your spouse will both learn more than you would studying alone. Besides, you may as well get used to it. Your spouse is going to be your missionary companion, and you need to start talking to each other about things other than kids, schedules, and money.

Finances

Speaking of money, it seems to be the cause of many of our pre-mission panic attacks. And there are some myths that just make the panic worse. No, you do not have to be completely out of debt to go on a mission. You do have to be able to pay for your mission and make your debt payments, though. No, you do not have to have your house paid off, but if you don't, you'd better have a way figured out to make your mortgage payments and still pay for your mission. No, you don't have to be rich to go on a mission. Some missions are relatively inexpensive, and others are relatively expensive. However, recently the Church has equalized things a great deal. They have put a cap of $1400 per month on the housing and utility expenses for all missions. That's the most you pay, not what all missions cost. For example, if you go on a temple mission, the housing costs are often very, very low, since many temples have living quarters associated with the temple.

Before you jump to any conclusions about missions and money, read chapter 5 in this book. It has the answers to frequently asked financial questions. Then go to the Missionary Service Opportunities Bulletin.[2] After pages and pages describing various mission opportunities, the last few pages list every country where there are missions and how much the monthly cost for that mission is. Note though, that these costs only include housing, utilities, food, supplies, transportation, and insurance. They do not include medical expenses, phone, Internet, clothing, or entertainment.

After you look over all the places you could afford to serve, you will have a better idea of how to organize your finances. You may decide to lease your home instead of letting the kids live there for free. Many couples decide to sell their home and move to something smaller when they return from their missions. But beware. More than a few couples have sold their home, only to find themselves waiting several months for visas.

And there are other financial considerations. You and your spouse may decide to officially retire and begin receiving Social Security payments. Your children may be willing to contribute a monthly portion of your mission costs. If one of your children is going to be responsible for paying your bills at home and you trust them, you may want to give them a signed power of attorney so they can do legal transactions for you if necessary.

When you fill out your mission application (see chapter 4), there is a small section on finances. They don't ask for your financial history or the amount of debt you have. They simply want to know how much you can pay each month and who will be paying what amount if others are contributing to your mission. Then they have a section where you can let them know anything else you want to about your finances. For example, you may want to say, "We plan to use Social Security payments to finance our mission."

What you do need to do early on is collect all your financial information, realistically decide how much you can afford to spend each month of your mission, and let the Church know on your application. They won't call you to a mission that you can't afford. Period.

Health

No, you can't leap tall buildings in a single bound. No, you are not twenty years old. No, you are not really all that healthy. You are, after all, a senior couple. It's important for you to understand that senior missionaries have different schedules and rules than junior missionaries—rules more suited to our venerable white hairs and creaky joints. There is absolutely no way you can be on task sixteen hours a day. Many of us can't even work eight hours a day.

However, the Church needs to know where you stand on your health. They want to know exactly which health problems you have had in the past and which ones you have now. They want to see all your medical records and medical history. Don't try to cover problems up. They won't use your information to prevent you from going on a mission. They will use it to help decide which mission will work best for you. Mainly, they need to know what level of medical care needs to be available to you as you serve. You can certainly serve a mission, even if you've had serious health problems in the past.

You won't be able to submit your papers until your doctor and dentist verify that you have no unresolved health issues that would prevent your serving a mission. One senior sister ended up needing twelve minor surgeries in the year before her mission, but she was definitely the exception and not the rule. If you know you need a crown on a tooth, get it now. If you know you need a hip replacement, start early. That way, when you're ready to apply for your mission, you won't have to wait for months to get medical appointments and recover from treatments or surgeries.

If you have chronic illnesses, such as diabetes or asthma, you need to get them stabilized and under control. Don't just hope they go away, because they won't. One senior elder ignored his diabetes and ended up in a crisis on his mission. It's not worth it. Just start now and get your health under control—at least as much as possible, given that everything seems to be sagging and creaking at our age.

By the way, don't get any special immunization shots until after you get your mission call. Different missions require different immunizations. Once you do get your call, however, jump right on the shots, because some have to be done in a series that may require several months to complete.

Marriage

Believe it or not, missions can put stress on your marriage. Yes, you may have been married for many years, but missions are different from regular married life. In most marriages, you mostly do your thing, and your spouse does his or her thing. Even most Church callings are separate and individual. When you do have a joint calling, you often split up the duties.

But on a mission, you are together a lot. And the way you have to interact may be different from anything you've done before. Some couples have to bite their tongues so that they won't bite off their spouse's head. "You didn't tell me . . ." "But I don't know how to . . ." "How come you always get to . . ." "That's not the way we planned . . ."

Before you begin your mission, you can do some preparation for the inevitable marriage adjustments. Do some tasks together: cook together, garden together, study together. And remember, it's all about trust and respect. (See chapter 15.)

Many, many couples discover that the tensions that exist initially on a first mission disappear in a few weeks. It's just figuring out how to roll with this new situation and how to put your relationship before any other single result, task, or expectation. Remember, you're both going to feel insecure and afraid. What you will really need is a strong dose of comfort, compliments, and patience.

By the way, the Church has produced a wonderful course called "Marriage and Family Relations." Before your mission, you might enjoy changing your family home evening habits— yes, you should be having family home evening even when you're old. It might be fun for you to get the marriage manual from lds.org[3] and study the eight lessons on strengthening marriage. It's never too late to learn how to have a happier marriage.

Skills

You may be terrified that you don't have the required language, computer, or communication skills that you think a mission will require. You may not be an extrovert. You may not be a good public speaker. It's tempting to say, "Forget it. I'm just not a mission kind of person, and I'm too old to learn new stuff."

Actually, there isn't a "mission kind of person." We tend to think a good missionary is a salesman type, a high-energy cheerleader, or a driven goal-setter. And we know we are just regular, quiet, insecure volunteers. So we decide to let some other high-profile couples do the senior mission thing. You'd be amazed to learn that your unique talent set can be just as effective as that of a high-powered person.

And the Lord knows you and your talents. He will put you where you can best use your abilities to help build His kingdom.

Nevertheless, there are some things you may choose to do before your mission to increase your skills. As you prepare to serve a mission, it's not necessary but it certainly wouldn't hurt you to begin learning the basics of the language your spouse learned on his or her junior mission. There is a reasonably good chance your senior mission calling will involve that language if you want to serve a foreign mission. The same goes for computer skills. Taking a basic word-processing or spreadsheet tutorial would be very helpful, even if you aren't actually called to serve in a mission office. And learning how to use email, Skype, Facebook, or other communication programs will be so easy and valuable as you try to stay in touch with your family. Get your grandkids to teach you to use the computer. You'll all have lots of laughs and make great memories.

The most effective thing you can do, though, is realistically look at what talents you have to offer just as you are. That evaluation would be fun to do with your spouse for a family home evening activity. Don't list your weaknesses and perceived problems. Just focus on your talents. And write the list down. You'll end up reading it over and over and treasuring it all your life.

Elder Nelson reassures: "Many humble Latter-day Saints fear that they are not qualified for missionary labors. But to such a prospective missionary, the Lord has given this assurance: 'Faith, hope, charity and love, with an eye single to the glory of God, qualify him for the work'"[4] (see D&C 4:5).

Conclusion

Elder Robert D. Hales said, "Just go and be yourselves."[5] In a later talk, he added,

> To those who were not able to serve a mission in their youth, may I speak directly to you. Perhaps over the years you have been burdened by feelings of regret or felt less than adequate because you did not have a missionary opportunity to serve and grow when you were younger. My advice to you: look forward, not back. Begin preparing for your mission as a senior missionary couple today! Save a little money each month. Study the scriptures. Accept Church callings. Pray to feel the Lord's love for others and receive His love and confidence in you. You can one day claim *all* the blessings of missionary service!

Then he exclaimed,

> My brothers and sisters, if you have felt stirrings to engage in this work, however quiet those feelings may be, do not procrastinate the day of your service. Now is the time to prepare; now is the time to be called, the time to sacrifice. Now is the time to share your gifts and talents, and now is the time to receive God's blessings for you and your family. . . . Let us, in our richest years of experience, maturity, wisdom, and most of all, our faith, rise to meet that need as only *we* can.[6]

Summary

Long before you are available to serve a mission, you can prepare by

- Studying the scriptures and *Preach My Gospel* together.
- Evaluating your financial situation and getting out of debt.

- Getting any health problems resolved or stabilized.
- Spending more time with your spouse working on tasks together.
- Learning or updating basic language and/or computer skills.
- Remembering that the Lord knows you and can use your talents to build His Kingdom.

Notes

1. Robert D. Hales, "Couple Missionaries: A Time to Serve," *Ensign*, May 2001.
2. www.lds.org/bc/content/ldsorg/callings/missionary/senior -missionary/senior-missionary-opportunities.pdf?lang=eng.
3. www.lds.org/manual/marriage-and-family-relations -instructors-manual?lang=eng.
4. Russell M. Nelson, "Senior Missionaries and the Gospel," *Ensign*, November 2004.
5. Hales, "Couple Missionaries: A Time to Serve."
6. Robert D. Hales, "Couple Missionaries: Blessings from Sacrifice and Service," *Ensign*, May 2005; emphasis in original.

Chapter 3

ON YOUR MARK, GET SET, APPLY!

Y ou've prayed, pondered, and prepared. You've felt the Spirit testify that it's time to serve a mission. So, where do you get the application papers? No, you can't go online and find the application anywhere. Even though it might sound fun to keep your application a secret and then surprise everyone when you get your call, that's not how the process works. When you're finally ready to serve, you have to make an appointment with your bishop and discuss your desires and feelings with him. Then he will use his authority to open a mission application for you.

From that point on, you are responsible for gathering information, completing the application, and getting all the medical approvals. This process will take some time, maybe even several months, so don't get discouraged when you start getting everything scheduled and bump into some roadblocks. The Church recommends that you begin filling out your Missionary Online Recommendation at least four months before the date you are available to start your mission, if you are serving inside your home country. If you are thinking of serving outside your home country, you should start applying at least six months before your availability date. However, your stake president may submit your application up to nine months before your availability date.

After your bishop has authorized your online mission application, you will need to use the Missionary Online Recommendation System at www.lds.org/mss to fill out your missionary recommendation. To access this system, you will need to have an LDS account ID and password. If you have been using FamilySearch, paying your tithing online, or using your online ward directory, then you use the same username and password as you do for those tasks. If not, it's easy to set up an account. Just make sure you choose a username and password that you can remember, because you'll use your LDS account for all kinds of projects and programs. Once you have an LDS account, you can go to www.lds.org/mss, sign in, and begin to answer the questions and follow the instructions. You will also need your membership record number, which is on your temple recommend or can be requested from your ward clerk.

Medical approvals can take extra time, especially if one or more of your tests raise a red flag. If that happens, and you need a further medical procedure, you can still submit your application before the procedure is complete. You just have to guarantee that the medical care will be done before you leave for your mission.

Just as a heads up, if you're not already up-to-date on your immunizations, as soon as you decide to serve a mission, you should begin the Hepatitis A and B immunization process because it takes six months to complete the immunization series. You will also need a tetanus shot, and if you were born after 1956, an MMR (Measles Mumps Rubella). Other immunization needs will depend on the country you are called to serve in.

Live-at-home missionaries are not required to have medical and dental examinations or to get immunizations.

When your application and all your medical forms are complete, you will return to your bishop for a final interview. He will fill in his recommendation on the application and then forward your completed application to the stake president, who will set up an interview with you. At that final interview, when everything is in order, the stake president will type his recommendation on the digital application and may then push the 'send' button right before your eyes. Finally, your application will magically land on the computers of the Missionary Committee, and the process of assigning you to a mission will begin.

Remember, though, that you are not in charge of where you will serve. As Elder David B. Haight cautioned,

> All missionary calls come from the Lord through inspiration to his servants. Therefore, it is not appropriate for couples to dictate where they will serve. President Howard W. Hunter said, "When we know *why* we serve, it won't matter *where* we serve!"
>
> However, we want to know as much as possible about potential couple missionaries, including what type of assignment they might like. When couple missionaries . . . apply to serve a mission, they fill out an additional form that provides us with such information as past employment experience, education or training, language skills, Church positions, special skills, abilities, interests, hobbies, and limitations or special circumstances. This information is considered when making assignments, as are age and health. Even couples who respond to openings listed in the "Church Service Missionary Opportunities"

bulletin may express their interest in a particular assignment, but the final decision still rests with the Brethren."[1]

Even if you are surprised or disappointed, if you accept the call you receive, you will discover that the Lord knows where your service is needed most and where you will benefit most by serving.

The Application

So let's take a detailed look at the missionary application you will be filling out. You're going to be giving the Missionary Committee a *lot* of information about yourself, but they will keep that information private and only use it to help them plan which missions you might best fit in. In fact, one of the things missionary couples often fail to do is give the committee *enough* information. You are encouraged to express your preferences on assignments and locations.

Most sections of the application have a place for you to give the committee additional information that wasn't asked for in the basic application. Use those sections to tell the committee about yourself and your talents and your limitations. Talk to them. Be honest. These people are there to serve you. If you withhold health information or limitations you may have, you are only making it more difficult for them to create a valid profile of you that the Apostles can use to make your call. Besides, this is a *mission* you are applying for. Do you want to try and fool the Lord? Give the committee all the information you can to help them help you.

Personal Information

The first thing you will fill in is your personal information: name, address, phone number, and birthday. They will also want to know about your citizenship, ancestry, and what your passport and driver's license numbers are.

Mission Preferences

Then they will want to know about your assignment preferences. Let's repeat the caution about preferences by quoting Elder Kent D. Watson of the Seventy: "In many cases they were surprised at the locations to which they were called. Some of them, perhaps like the prophet Jonah, may have chosen Tarshish over Nineveh, as it were. But they did not 'flee unto Tarshish from the presence of the Lord' or reside 'in the belly of the fish three days and three nights' (Jonah 1:3, 17). Rather, knowing their calls came from the Lord, 'they straightway left their nets, and followed him' (Matthew 4:20)."[2]

We know of a couple that thought they had their call all set. The husband spoke Portuguese, and they wanted to serve in Portugal. So they called the mission president in Lisbon. He said he would love to have them serve with him, and he sent a request into the Missionary Committee. On their application, they put that they had arranged with the Portuguese mission president to serve with him. Then they submitted their application, figuring there would be no surprises. But when they opened their call, they were flabbergasted to find that they had been called to New Zealand!

There are many different types of missions that couples can investigate. As Elder Russell M. Nelson summarizes, "Categories include leadership and member work; family history and temple service; medical, humanitarian, and welfare services; working at visitors' centers, for public affairs, on an area or mission office staff, with finance and records, with physical facilities, for the Church Educational System, with the Perpetual Education Fund, or in support of other educational endeavors. Other opportunities are available to suit the unique abilities possessed by prospective missionaries."[3] Elder Kent D. Watson adds,

> Some of their numerous and diverse assignments include working in temples, teaching seminary and institute, serving in mission offices, administering the Perpetual Education Fund, serving in branches . . . , mentoring and helping people upgrade job skills and enhance employment, working in their professional specialties (law, finance, engineering, education, health care), coordinating humanitarian services, and providing relief during floods, earthquakes, and other natural disasters. Some of them even get to participate in finding, teaching, and baptizing new members![4]

The two most common missionary assignments, according to the missionary bulletin, are member and leader support missions and mission office couple assignments. Here is how the bulletin describes these two assignments.

Member and Leader Support (MLS)

> Member and leader support (MLS) is the most common type of assignment for senior missionary couples called to serve under the direction of a mission president. This assignment encourages couples to share the gospel, reactivate and rescue less-active members, retain new converts, strengthen young single adults, and support local leaders in struggling wards, branches, and districts. Couples also provide a great and lasting influence on younger missionaries serving within a mission. Only couples may serve as member and leadership support missionaries.[5]

Mission Office Couples

"Senior missionary couples with experience using Microsoft Word and Excel are needed to serve as office couples. Office assignments include secretary to the mission president, financial secretary, apartment administrators, vehicle fleet administrators, and referral secretaries. In addition, senior missionaries with office assignments may help with member and leader support (MLS) assignments in the evenings and on weekends."[6] Couples are needed to serve in mission office assignments around the world to allow mission presidents to minister and focus on missionaries, instead of administrative duties.

But even though these assignments are the most common, you should look at the opportunities listed in the missionary bulletin before you turn in your application. You'll be surprised at the variety of missions available. Some missionaries take care of landscaping. Some do plumbing. Some make candles at Nauvoo and dance in the evenings. Whether you choose to serve a foreign mission or not, it's really fun to read about all the options. If one of the opportunities looks intriguing, contact the person listed under that opportunity, and they will let you know what is involved. Then they will help you let the committee know of your interest in that area.

This is one of those sections that has space for you to give the committee extra information, so use it to explain your interests and limitations. Your input does matter and is considered as they put together your profile.

Finances

The finance section of the application just asks how much you can afford to pay each month for your mission so that the committee won't assign you to a mission that will be impossible for you to pay for. Again, be honest. This section has a space for you to explain any financial information you want considered.

Availability

In general, you can choose to serve a six-month, twelve-month, eighteen-month, or twenty-three-month mission. Do take the time to consider this choice prayerfully and carefully. The Church wants you to serve according to your abilities. You won't be a "slacker" if you choose to serve eighteen months instead of twenty-three months. No one will judge you or raise their eyebrows if you go home earlier than they do. Just be wise and thoughtful as you make this decision.

Some of the specialty mission assignments have a designated time of service. For example, if one of you is going to serve as an auditor, you may be required to serve for twenty-three months. If your assignment takes a while to learn, you may not be given a six-month option because you would be returning home just about the time you finally figured out how to do the job. But the time requirement will be explained to you when you call to find out more information about specialty missions. For those missions, you fill in the designated time in this section.

The option to serve for six or twelve months is available in foreign missions, but only if you pay your own transportation to and from the mission. We suppose that's part of the reason why most couples choose to serve for eighteen or twenty-three months.

There is also a space to discuss special circumstances about the length of your mission. Use it if you have any concerns at all. Remember, these brothers and sisters are your friends.

You will also be asked to provide the date you will be available to begin your mission.

Life Experiences

This is a really fun section that reminds you of all the things you have learned to do throughout your life. You may be a very good truck driver, mechanic, teacher, manager, photographer, programmer, writer, plumber, genealogist, homemaker, cook, dancer, cheerleader, counselor, adviser, gardener, or choir director. The list of skills for you to choose from is long and varied. They give you three levels of expertise for each skill, so you have some flexibility.

They also want to know your work history and educational and professional background. This section is just one long paragraph you write telling them what you've done professionally in your life. The Church doesn't care if you have a PhD or not, but if you do happen to be a master engineer, they would like to know that. Even then, there's no guarantee you'll use that degree on your mission. Chances are you won't. But what if the Church desperately needed a dental hygienist just at the moment you applied and that's your specialty?

The application also has space for you to report any other special skills you have that may not be listed.

The committee also wants to know what foreign language skills you may have and what level of skill you still have. Remember, if you spoke Danish forty years ago on your mission, you probably aren't fluent unless you've been speaking it regularly since then. But any language skills can be helpful. If you want to learn a foreign language, you might get the chance. However, as a senior, you may be surprised at how challenging that new language is, no matter how smart you are.

And finally, in this section, they want to know about all your Church experiences—callings, previous missions, leadership experiences, temples you have served in, and so on.

Health Insurance

In order to serve a mission, you must have health insurance. If you are serving a foreign mission, that health insurance must be in addition to Medicare because Medicare doesn't cover expenses you incur outside the United States. So if you don't have insurance, the Church lets you purchase relatively inexpensive insurance. However, there is no such thing as inexpensive health insurance, so be prepared for some sticker shock. After all, both of you are older now, so you are a bigger risk for the insurance companies.

Health History

This section is so detailed and long that you will be amazed and perhaps dismayed. The committee wants to know about every single health problem you now have *or have ever had.* Then they want you to explain how you are dealing with each of your current health problems.

No one wants to admit that they have health problems, so they tend to minimize their responses or just flat out ignore the truth about their health. That's why the Church actually added a caution at the first of this section, to be honest. Remember, the Church needs you and wants you to serve a mission. They just don't want you stuck in Bora Bora with no way to get your cancer treated because you didn't mention on your application that you had cancer a couple of years ago.

Missions are not easy, but some are physically quite a lot harder than others. So give the committee a fair chance as they try to create your profile. Explain problems you've had and what you are doing to accommodate those problems. Some of us simply can't serve a mission that requires extensive standing or walking, but we can still serve in an office. Don't try to psyche out the committee or minimize your realities. Just tell them what your limitations and health problems are and have faith that Heavenly Father has a place for you to serve. We know of a young elder who was paralyzed from his chest down and still served a mission. We met a senior sister who served her mission in a wheelchair. You have much to offer, even if your body is not as spry as it once was.

Medical Reports

Along with your application, you will have to submit reports from your doctor and from your dentist that verify that you are healthy enough to serve a mission. To get these reports, you will have to print out documents in your application that you will then take to your appointments. Your doctor will have to do a bunch of lab tests and other tests to see if things are reasonably normal. Then your doctor will have to wait for the test results before they will sign your mission release form. Your dentist will want to make sure your teeth are in good shape and will update any work you need to have done. In our experience, dental problems are the most common health problems senior missionaries have while they are in the field. Those old teeth and old fillings just don't hold up as well as you'd wish they would. So get any necessary dental work done before you leave.

Now all of this takes a bit of time, especially if one or more of your lab tests come out iffy. So prepare to wait awhile for all of this medical stuff to get processed. Just print off the forms and make the appointments as soon as you can. Then let the process run its course. Eventually you will have the medical releases in hand and ready to submit with your application.

Photo

You will need to include a photo of you and your spouse in your application, and this photo is fairly important. It will be used by the General Authorities when they decide where you should be called to serve. They will use your photo to help them see you as God sees you. Your photo will also be used by your mission president all through your mission. It will be posted on his missionary board along with the photos of all the other missionaries in your mission.

So take some care with your photo. The photo dimensions and instructions are designated in your mission application. Essentially, you will be sending a head shot of the two of you. Your photo doesn't have to be done by a professional, but it should be of good quality. Dress in missionary clothing, including suit and tie, missionary haircuts and hairstyles, with no beard or mustache. It's nice for your photo to show that you like each other, so do smile and let your spirit shine through.

Permissions

At the end of your application, you will be asked to sign various privacy agreements, disclosures, documents, releases, and acknowledgments that protect you and the Church. Don't worry about these agreements—the Church simply wants to get your permission to collect and process your information. Your privacy will be preserved.

Documents

Finally, the Church wants copies of the front pages of your passport and the front and back of your driver's license scanned into your computer and attached to your application. You may need to get your kids or grandkids to help you get these documents scanned and attached if you're like most of us. Never fear. They won't even bat an eye at the task. Computer skills are like breathing to them. No kids or grandkids close? The teenagers in your ward will be thrilled to help you out. Besides, it's a good idea to get familiar with scanning and begin brushing up on your computer skills.

Conclusion

So that's it. You've got your application filled out. You've got your medical releases in hand. You've got your documents scanned. You're set to return to your bishop and get interviewed. He'll send your application to the stake, and then you'll wait to hear from the stake clerk so you can make an appointment with the stake president. If you haven't heard from the stake clerk in about a week, call your bishop and find out what the status of your application is. He has access to a computer program that will trace your application from the time he sends it from his computer to the date the Church mails your call.

Sometimes people push the wrong button or forget to enter an application properly, so don't hesitate to check with your bishop if you want to know what's happening with your application. He'll understand that you are sitting on pins and needles, and he'll let you know the status of your application.

Here's an important warning, though. Although junior missionaries get their calls about two weeks from when the stake president pushes the 'send' button, it takes five or six weeks for seniors to receive their calls. That's because senior applications have a *lot* more information for the committee to compile and contemplate. After all, you've lived a lot longer than those junior kids. So be patient. Your call will come, and it will be the call Heavenly Father has in mind for you to best build His kingdom.

In Elder Robert D. Hales's words, "I testify that as we put our trust in the Lord, He will find the right missionary opportunity for us. As He said, 'If any man serve me, him will my Father honor.'"[7]

Summary

- Your bishop is the only person that can initiate your missionary application.
- You should apply for your mission four to six months before your availability date.
- You will need both medical and dental clearances before your application can be submitted.
- The application will ask for detailed information about your health, your experiences, and your interests.
- The application will provide numerous opportunities for you to add comments. Use them.
- You can state your mission preferences in your application, but your call will come from the Lord.
- After your stake president sends in your application, it can take five to six weeks to receive your call.

Notes

1. David B. Haight, "Couple Missionaries—'A Wonderful Resource,'" *Ensign*, February 1996; italics in original.

2. Kent D. Watson, "Our Senior Missionaries," *Ensign*, September 2010.

3. Russell M. Nelson, "Senior Missionaries and the Gospel," *Ensign*, November 2004, footnote 12, referencing Giles H. Florence Jr., "So Many Kinds of Missions," *Ensign*, February 1990.

4. Kent D. Watson, "Our Senior Missionaries," *Ensign*, September 2010.

5. *Senior Missionary Opportunities Bulletin* (The Church of Jesus Christ of Latter-day Saints, November 23, 2016), 4, https://www.lds.org/bc/content/ldsorg/callings/missionary/senior-missionary/senior-missionary-opportunities.pdf.

6.   Ibid.

7.   Robert D. Hales, "Couple Missionaries: Blessings from Sacrifice and Service," *Ensign*, May 2005.

Chapter 4

YOUR CALL IS HERE—NOW WHAT?

It finally came! Your call has arrived in the mail. Your call letter will tell you what mission you are serving in, how long you are called to serve, what kind of mission assignment you have been given, and when and where you are to report to begin your mission.

Some people open their call immediately. Some have a special family home evening with their children and grandchildren. Some people even videotape the opening of their call. But no matter how you choose to discover where you will be spending your mission, as soon as you find out, you will probably rush to the computer. Where exactly is Birmingham, Alabama, or Luanda, Angola? What is the weather like there? What do they eat? How do they dress? What does our assignment entail? Where can I get answers to all my questions?

Take a deep breath and try to stay calm. There are answers. This time of preparation is one of the most exciting times of your life, so enjoy it and savor the thrilling experiences you are about to have.

You will be amazed at how much information you can get from your computer search engine. You can type in "LDS mission Moscow, Russia," and you will get lots of websites to visit. Then you can click links from one website to another. You will find blogs from senior couples who have returned from the very mission you were called to. You will find maps and cultural information. You will find photos and stories. Just remember that you are using the Internet, so not all the information you find may be valid. Write down questions you think of as you investigate or you will forget what you want to find out. After all, you are a senior missionary, so you have a senior memory, and your mind may be particularly fragmented during this initial excitement. But remember, the Church has lots of reliable resources for you.

Within a very few days of receiving your call, you will begin to receive information from the Church Missionary Committee and from your mission president. You will also be contacted by a senior missionary couple who has been assigned to answer your questions and support you.

From the Missionary Committee, you will receive a packet in the mail that will tell you about general guidelines, clothing standards, visa requirements, and preparation details. Your whole attention will probably be on the pictures they send of recommended clothing, and you're going to want to immediately rush off to the store and begin putting together outfits. (See chapter 8 before you buy one single thing!) But try to contain your enthusiasm for just a few moments. First things first, and those first things for couples going to foreign missions are visas and passports. Do not even think of stepping into a store until you have applied for these two important documents. Besides, your specific mission clothing guidelines may differ from the general guidelines. Make sure you wait to receive the information packet from your mission president before you start collecting your missionary wardrobe.

Visas

Depending on the country you are serving in, getting a visa can take from three months to a year. The Missionary Travel Office will send you the correct visa forms and requirements, and they will be available to answer any questions you have. But getting a visa can be challenging. Sometimes visas are so hard to get that your mission call must be changed to a different mission.

So what is a visa, anyway? A visa is permission from the government of a country to allow you to stay in their country for more than a few weeks or months to work as a missionary. Students must obtain student visas to study in foreign countries. Some people get work visas so they can work in their company's international office. Countries guard their borders carefully and only allow a few foreigners to stay for an extended time. If the US is restricting visas for citizens of a certain country, that country may restrict visas to US citizens in return. But beyond that, there are all sorts of other reasons for delayed visas that you have no control over.

What you do have control over is getting your visa application submitted to the Missionary Travel Office as soon as possible. A missionary visa packet explaining the details of your visa application will usually arrive two weeks after your mission call letter. Someone from the Missionary Travel Office will contact you and begin working with you to get all your papers submitted. Visa applications are country specific. Many require certified birth certificates. If you don't have one, you can look online for the state vital records office and call them. They will charge you for a certified copy of your birth certificate, and they will probably have an option to get an expedited certificate for a bit more money. Do it. Time is of the essence for your visa.

Some countries require an original or official marriage certificate, and you will need to contact the state that you were married in and get an official marriage certificate. Some visa applications require official educational transcripts or proof of religious instruction, which can be a real pain in the neck. Ask the Missionary Committee how to get your seminary and institute transcripts. It is possible, because we've done it.

Most visa applications will want an FBI report, local police department report, and digital fingerprints—not ink ones. You can get the fingerprints and report from your local police department, but call them to make sure. The FBI report can be a real bottleneck. We've seen it take months to get that report. There are services that will expedite this report for a fee, and it's worth every penny. You can find them online or from the travel department.

Get your visa application put together and submitted to the Missionary Travel Office as soon as possible so that they can send your application to the appropriate consulate to process.

Passports

If you don't already have a passport that is valid until six months after the end of your mission, apply for one as soon as you get your call. As a rule, passports take several months to get and cost over $100. However, if you spend an extra $60 or so, you can get one sooner.

You can apply for a passport at your local post office or county clerk's office. Check online. But do apply before you renew your driver's license. (See Driver's Licenses on the following page.)

Once you receive your passport, make two photocopies of the passport ID page for security purposes. If you lose your passport or it is stolen, you'll be glad you have these copies.

Just a side note—when you submit your passport and your visa application to the Missionary Travel Office, they will keep your passport until your visa arrives, which can be several months. If you plan to travel outside the US before leaving on your mission, let the Missionary Committee know. They will let you send your passport in after your trip. But they will need it, because they have to paste your visa right into your passport before you can use it for your mission. Normally, you will get your passport with the visa pasted in it while you are at the MTC.

Driver's Licenses

Even if you go to a foreign country, you should have a valid driver's license. Many countries honor US driver's licenses.

If your driver's license is going to expire some time during your mission, you will need to renew it before you leave the country. Trying to renew your license from abroad is just overwhelmingly difficult and takes a great deal of time and effort. So look at your driver's license right away and see if you'll need to renew it before you start your mission.

You have to jump through some special hoops to renew a license that doesn't expire fairly soon. When you go to the Department of Motor Vehicles (DMV) in your area, make sure you bring two acceptable forms of ID. Your local DMV website will list which forms of ID are acceptable, but your current, valid driver's license and your passport work well, as long as you haven't already sent your passport to the Missionary Travel Office. Some DMVs require a birth certificate. Ours required a copy of our mission call! We had to go clear back home to get it. Grr. So you may want to telephone ahead and make sure you have all the documents your DMV will require for early renewal.

Temple Recommend

Don't worry about renewing your temple recommend early. Your mission president can renew it for you while you're on your mission.

Resources

For any questions you can't find answers to in the Church missionary websites, email SeniorMissionaryServices@ ldschurch.org.

For information on dress and grooming standards, go to www.missionaryclothing.lds.org.

The Church Missionary Department can be contacted directly by telephone. Email Senior Missionary Services to obtain the phone numbers for medical insurance information, travel information, passport and visa information, medical information, specific assignment information, financial preparation information, or electronic device information.

For frequently asked questions, here is another great resource: https://beta.lds.org/bc/content/shared/content/english /pdf/missionary/senior-missionaries-faq-17-12-2000.pdf.

And you might find the Missionary Handbook helpful, though it is mostly geared to junior missionaries: www.lds.org /manual/missionary-handbook?lang=eng.

Your Specific Mission Information

About a week after you receive your call, your assigned mission will send you a packet of information that is specific to your mission. It will include information about what you will need to bring (umbrella and raincoat, or not, for example), what your housing situation will be, whether you will have access to a car, what the electric voltage is in your country, what electronic devices will work in your country (cell phone or not, for example), and lots more. (See chapter 9 for more information about electronic devices and electric appliances.)

Once you receive your mission packet, you will be able to email the mission office couple and get lots more information on specific questions you may have. If for some reason the packet doesn't have the mission office email address, just ask the Senior Missionary Services (SeniorMissionaryServices@ ldschurch.org) what the office email address is.

Most of us sisters will correspond with the senior office sister many, many times as we prepare for our missions. It's amazing how many weird questions you'll think of. You may want to know about what jewelry to bring, what kind of temple garments the sisters find most comfortable, what medications are available, whether your brand of mascara is available, and on, and on. But don't worry. You'll have months of preparation time between the week you get your call and the day you actually fly out to start your mission.

Travel

Traveling to your mission can be extremely long and exhausting. (See chapter 11.) If you have special travel needs, such as needing a wheelchair at the airport, be sure to let the Missionary Travel Office know months before you enter the MTC. In my case, the travel department automatically assumes that I will want to sit by my husband during my flight to my mission. However, since I hate to sit in a middle seat on airlines and really need to lean against the window with my inflatable cushions, I need a window seat. But my husband wants an aisle seat. We don't care if a stranger sits between us, but we always hope the middle seat will remain empty.

Normally, when I fly, I just get online and choose the seats I want for a flight. In this case, since the Missionary Travel Office is purchasing and controlling your plane tickets, they are the only ones that can select your seats. So, if you have special seating needs, you can call the travel department, and they will try to set up seats that you will like. However, you will need to let them know of your needs soon after you receive your initial packet from them.

Summary

- After you receive your call, you will be assigned a senior missionary support couple.
- Within a week or so, you will receive a packet of information from the Church Missionary Committee.
- You will also receive a packet of information from your specific mission office.
- If you are going to a foreign country, you will need to get a passport and visa.
- If your driver's license will expire on your mission, you will need to renew it before you leave.
- You can renew your temple recommend in the mission field.
- The Missionary Travel Office will buy your plane tickets and deliver them to you in the MTC.

Chapter 5

MONEY MATTERS

Talking about money and worrying about all the financial details of missions is *so* boring. But you really need to know some practical information *before* you leave your home country or state and venture into a different place. You have to consider questions like "What are we going to do with our house?," "How are we going to pay our bills when we're away?," and "Who do we send our mission housing payment to?"

So this chapter is full of basic mission money advice. Let's start at the very beginning.

What is your mission going to cost?

Junior missionaries all over the world pay the same amount every month for their missions, no matter where they serve, but that isn't true for senior missionaries. Remember, when you applied for your mission, you told the committee how much you could afford to pay and who was going to help you meet your mission costs. Also remember that the mission costs were listed for each mission near the end of the Senior Missionary Bulletin (www.lds.org/senioropportunities). The bulletin's estimated cost for you as a couple for your mission includes the following:

- Housing—Includes rent, utilities, all furnishings, fees, and parking (the total of which will not exceed $1,400 for couples).
- Personal—Consumables, food, personal care (bath supplies, office supplies, laundry, haircuts, and so on).
- Transportation—Personal auto operating costs, car rental and fuel (for some missions), or public transportation costs.

The bulletin's estimated cost does *not* include the following:

- Communications—Internet, cable/satellite TV, telephone service, or personal cell phone.
- Medical Care—Prescription drugs, over-the-counter medications and supplies, or physician care.
- Other—Gifts, charitable giving, clothing, personal obligations, entertainment, and so on.

So you and your spouse need to sit down and figure out how much money you will need every month during your mission. Don't forget to include expenses like tithing and offerings (discussed below), bills you have to pay at home, and other obligations you have committed to.

The great news is that many of us have found that we spent far less per month while we were serving our missions than we usually did at home. But, of course, some couples have plenty of money, so they buy lots of souvenirs, go to expensive restaurants, and attend the opera (if there is one in their city). For us, it was just the basics, and the basics can be pretty cheap. That said, I really missed the great sales you can find in the US on groceries and supplies.

Who do you pay your mission obligation to, and how do you pay it when you're away from home?

a. You pay your basic monthly mission fee every month to your ward mission fund. This fee only covers your mission housing and utilities. To make your donation, go to lds.org and click "My Account and Ward" in the upper right corner. The site will have you log in with your username and password—the same ones you used to apply for your mission. Then, under the heading "My Account and Ward" and the subheading "My Ward," click "Donations." On the donation slip that is shown, go to "Ward Mission Fund" and click the arrow on the side. Your name will appear in the alphabetical list of missionaries serving from your ward. Click your name and then fill in the amount you have been asked to pay monthly. Then continue through the series of pages until your donation is complete. The money will be taken out of the bank account you have listed with the Church.

b. If you don't want to use the online donation system, *before you leave*, you can set up an automatic bill pay service with your bank. Have them send a monthly check to your ward, *using your bishop's home address*. Then your ward financial clerk will enter the payment into the ward's system.

c. Or you can have a family member make the payments to your ward.

Remember, your ward is being billed for your mission, so they need your donation on time every month.

And a side note—it's better to pay each month than pay several months or more at a time. There is a chance that one of you may get sick and need to end your mission early, and you won't be able to get your donations refunded. Because these donations are nonrefundable, they are tax deductible.

How do I pay tithing and fast offerings?

a. You can use the online donation system to pay your tithing or you can set up a bill pay service with your bank as described in step b above.

b. You are not expected to pay tithing on any funds you receive for your mission from your family, ward, stake, or others.

c. You pay fast offerings to the ward or branch where you serve your mission.

Do I have to be out of debt before I can go on a mission?

It's not an absolute requirement, but being out of debt, especially consumer debt like credit cards and installment loans, is highly encouraged. If you do have any debt, you need to have a solid arrangement for making the payments. The last thing you want to worry about on your mission is whether your car is going to get repossessed while you're gone.

What do I do with my home while I'm on my mission?

You have several options for dealing with your home:

a. You can have a family member or friend live in your home.

b. You can lease or rent your home to someone.

c. You can sell your home and buy something else when you return.

d. You can leave your home vacant and have someone care for it and the yard.

Some Important Notes:

1. *Before you sell, rent, lease, or leave* your home to someone else, make sure you have received your visa and that your MTC date is finalized. Visas can take from 60 to 150 days or more to process, and they often take longer than you plan. We know of couples who sold their homes and found themselves living in a motel while they waited for their visas to arrive.

2. *Before you leave,* if you are going to leave your home empty, make sure someone is willing to check on it frequently and maintain the yard. Also advise your insurance company and check on your coverage.

3. *Before you leave,* make sure you deal with how your utilities and other housing expenses are going to be handled.

4. If no one will be driving your cars while you're gone, you may be able to get the cost of your car insurance drastically reduced during your mission. Check with your insurance company.

What about paying my taxes?

If your taxes are basic and simple, you can pay your taxes while you are on your mission by using an online tax program. Some of the programs are even free. However, if your taxes require multiple schedules and complex figuring, you need to hire a tax advisor *before* you leave on your mission and make sure he or she has all the papers, forms, and income information they will need.

As a great side note, any mission fund donations you make to your ward mission fund and possibly some of your mission expenses may be tax deductible. Check with your tax advisor.

What do I need to know about credit cards, debit cards, and banks?

Advise Your Bank

Before you leave, let your bank know that you will be serving a mission, where you be serving, and how long you'll be away. Otherwise, when they see charges coming through from a foreign country or different state, they may panic and lock your account. That's a real pain to deal with, especially if your day is their night and you can't talk to them easily. You probably won't need to open a new bank account in your mission state or country.

Lost or Stolen Cards

Before you leave, make sure you have two accounts that have credit and debit cards. Your bank card may be stolen, hacked, or lost. If that happens, you must immediately cancel the card and let your bank know what happened. That way, they can void fraudulent charges. If that happens, you will have the card from the second account to use when your primary card is canceled.

If you don't set up two accounts, once you cancel your bank card, you have no way to buy food or other things, and it can take a *long* time to get a new card, if you can get one at all. Especially in developing countries, mail service is unreliable.

Moreover, your bank usually will only send a replacement card to the home address you have listed on your account. And when you try to activate the new card, they will not allow you to use a phone that is not listed on your account.

So, the easiest thing to do is to store a card for the second account in a safe place in your apartment or mission office. Having a second card on your main account won't help a bit, since they close all card access to that account.

If you do need to replace a lost or stolen card, you will need someone you trust to collect your new card from your home mail, activate it *before* they send it to you, and then send it using a service like DHL, FedEx, or UPS. Those services cost a lot, but at least you'll have access to your account.

We kept a minimal amount in the account for the card we used all the time so that if it was hacked, our losses would be minimal. It's easy to transfer money from one bank account to another if you have the bank set it up *before* you leave.

Chip-and-PIN Cards

The new chip-and-PIN type of bank card is much more secure than the old swipe kind of card, so if your bank offers the chip-and-PIN card, it's a good idea to get one and test it before you go to make sure it works properly. Unlike many places in the US, foreign countries prefer that you use the chip-and-PIN kind of card.

Card Safety

Your credit card is your money lifeline, but it is really vulnerable to fraud. Here are some safety hints, especially if you are serving in a developing country.

1. Never allow your card to be out of your sight. Don't give your card to a waiter to take away and process. They can process the card at your table. Don't let a cashier process your card away or under a table. Watch your card the entire time it is being processed.
2. Never let someone "help" you at an ATM.
3. Don't use an ATM that is in an out-of-the-way place or that is isolated, and don't use an ATM that you haven't seen work successfully. But don't use an ATM that has lots of people crowding around it either.
4. Don't let people see your PIN number.
5. Watch out for pickpockets.
6. Don't carry your card in a wallet or purse.

That's a lot of information, and some of it is scary, but you should be fine if you set up your home and bank processes before you leave on your mission.

Conclusion

Remember, the Lord wants you to serve a mission, and He will help you work things out. Listen to Sister Brunhilde Gehrmann: "When we considered going on a mission, we had concerns. . . . Our little house couldn't be rented, and there were financial worries. We discussed it together and spoke about all the pros and cons. But in the end we knelt down and asked our Father in Heaven for guidance. After that it was very easy. We both had a good feeling and the certainty that we should go on a mission."[1]

Take heart. There are many people, both on earth and in heaven, who will come to your aid.

Elder Robert D. Hales said,

"In considering missionary opportunities, many couples throughout the world have an abundant desire to serve but lack abundant means. If this is your situation, remember that the right mission call may not be to a far-off country with a strange sounding name. The right call for you may be within your stake or area. 'Your heavenly Father knoweth that ye have need of all these things.' Counsel with your extended family and your bishop or branch president. As the Lord's servants understand your temporal situation, you will be able to receive the eternal blessings of full-time missionary service.'"[2]

Summary

- You should know about what your mission will cost before you even apply.
- You pay your monthly mission obligation to your home ward using a donation slip.
- While on your mission, you pay your tithing to your home ward and your fast offering to your local ward or branch.
- You should plan what to do with your home well in advance before leaving on your mission.
- You must pay US taxes while you are on your mission.
- You should advise your bank where you will be serving and for how long.
- You should set up a second bank account with its own cards and have the bank make it possible for you to transfer money from one account to another.
- Safeguard your bank card, especially in developing countries.

Notes

1. Brunhilde Gehrmann, "Mission Blessings in the Golden Years," *Ensign*, December 2005.
2. Robert D. Hales, "Couple Missionaries: Blessings from Sacrifice and Service," *Ensign*, May 2005.

Chapter 6

HEALTH CONCERNS

Yes, you're getting older. Your body is sagging. Your hair is thinner. And all those new wrinkles! But your appearance issues are minor compared to your real health problems. You may be asking, "Can I really serve a mission if I have a weak heart or diabetes? What if I have had cancer in the past?" The answer is a resounding, "Yes, you can!"

There are so many different kinds of missionary service for senior couples. Some missions require lots of physical activity, and some don't. Some countries have great medical services available, and some don't. That's why it is so important for you to give the Missionary Committee complete and accurate information about your health history and concerns. (See chapter 4.)

Because I have fibromyalgia, on my first mission application, I explained, "I can't stand for more than a few moments; I can't sit for very long and never in a bad chair; I can't bend and hold that position; I can't kneel or squat; I can't hold my arms up or out." Later, my mission president in Portugal laughed, "When I read that, I asked myself, 'I wonder what she *can* do!'" But when we arrived in the mission office, he was amazed at all the work I got done quickly and effectively. After all, I *could* type fast. I *could* use the computer well. I *could* organize the office and maintain missionary records. And I *could* nurture the missionaries and make sure their apartments were clean and well maintained.

Realistically, we all have disabilities of one kind or another. Some are easy to see, and some are less obvious, but equally disabling. Heavenly Father knows who we are. He knows our strengths and our weaknesses, and He can use us to build His kingdom throughout the world. Remember what He tells us in Ether 12:27: "I give unto men weakness that they may be humble; and my grace is sufficient for all men that humble themselves before me; for if they humble themselves before me, and have faith in me, then will I make weak things become strong unto them."

So lift up your hearts and be glad. You, too, can serve a mission, even if you feel old, tired, and decrepit. Elder David B. Haight reminds us: "Couples are not expected to work as many hours as the younger missionaries. Couples have many varied talents and are to prudently work to their strength and abilities. They are not expected to do more than they are able. Most couples have some limitations based on age and health. If they need to rest occasionally, they may do so."[1]

In a talk from Elder Kent D. Watson, Sister Brenda Frandsen explains: "Perhaps one of my biggest fears was health concerns; instead, we have experienced health blessings. Our missionary schedule is healthful. We get up early, retire early, exercise daily, and eat nutritious foods. The Lord blesses missionaries with strength to perform their labors. You need not be afraid!"[2]

So now, let's address some specific health questions senior couples may have.

If I need surgery, should I wait to submit my mission application?

Yes. You will need a release form from your doctor that says you are ready to serve. There is no need to rush out to the mission field and then be laid up with health problems. Take care of or stabilize any problems before you submit your papers.

Do I need to have a colonoscopy and/or mammogram?

These procedures are recommended for all senior missionaries, and they are required for those planning to serve outside their home country.

Do I need to have a cardiac stress test?

You do if you have several risk factors and plan to serve outside your home country.

What immunizations will I need?

Normally, all senior missionaries need the following immunizations:

- Hepatitis A and B (since this series takes six months to complete, you should start it as soon as you decide to serve a mission)
- Tetanus
- MMR, if you were born after 1956.

Other immunizations may be required for specific mission assignments.

Make sure to have your immunization record filled out and signed for each immunization you receive. You'll need to take this card with you to the MTC and to your mission country to prove that you have received the immunizations required.

How can I get medications if I am serving outside the US?

You can bring a supply of medications with you to start, and if the mail service is reliable in your country, you can have subsequent refills mailed to you. We have found, however, that it is easiest to simply visit a local doctor and get prescriptions filled at a local pharmacy. Pharmacies often won't accept prescriptions from doctors who are out of state or out of country, especially if the prescriptions are for controlled substances. Some controlled substances are illegal in certain countries, so you may not be able to serve there.

Don't be misled by well-meaning people who say you won't need prescriptions for medications in developing countries. You probably will, and you will need to get those prescriptions from local doctors. Check with your mission office to see if specific medications are available in your mission.

Will my insurance cover medical procedures, doctor visits, and medications on my mission?

Medicare only covers you in the US. That's why the Church requires senior missionaries serving in other countries to have additional medical insurance. Generally, though, these insurance companies will not directly pay providers in foreign countries. You have to pay the providers yourself and then submit your receipts for reimbursement. Check with your insurance company to see what their regulations and restrictions are. Some require you to submit your receipts within a certain number of months after the service is provided.

What medical insurance do I have to have?

Even if the country you are going to has a national health program, every senior missionary must have health insurance coverage. You are not allowed to use the national health program unless you are a permanent resident of that country. Senior missionaries are older, so their bodies tend to fall apart more easily. Medical insurance coverage is so important to the Church that if your insurance coverage is cancelled for any reason and you don't get another, you will be reassigned to a mission in your home country or be released early!

If you already have health insurance other than Medicare, great. But if you don't, the Church has arranged with Deseret Mutual Benefit Administrators (DMBA) to offer medical insurance policies. You can get details about this program at www.dmba.com/ssmp. There are no restrictions based on health history or preexisting conditions.

Coverage with this company begins the day you begin your mission, as defined in your mission call letter, and ends the day of your release. However, DMBA's Senior Service Medical Plan provides up to ninety days post-mission transitional coverage if you notify them when you initially sign up.

Live-at-home missionaries are not required to have medical insurance.

Since Medicare doesn't work in foreign countries, can I suspend my payments while I'm serving outside the US?

You can, but it's a real hassle. You have to work with both Social Security and Medicare, and they don't understand this particular regulation very well. However, if you have DMBA insurance, they can provide consultation and assistance in the Medicare disenrollment and reenrollment process.

Conclusion

Finally, while you are serving your mission, you will be the steward of your health. You will need to monitor your personal energy and physical condition. Don't just ignore warning signs of health problems, whether physical or mental. Such issues certainly won't simply get better by themselves! Get medical help early and save yourself a lot of grief.

And as a wise steward, you know you need to eat nutritious food every single day. You need to take the time to cook balanced meals. You need to take a multivitamin. You need to exercise every day—it's even in the Missionary Handbook. You need to take time to rest and rejuvenate. You and your spouse need to go on dates and take time to counsel together. Your personal health is so important that it is mentioned throughout the scriptures. So take care of yourself. And be aware of your spouse's health too.

Now, sometimes, in spite of your best efforts, your health just falls apart and you have to deal with serious health problems. Sometimes senior missionaries have senior-sized health issues. Often, those health problems can be dealt with right in your mission. One senior missionary had his appendix out in Africa, but the health care facilities in his city were exceptionally good. One of our relatives discovered she had cancer just three months into her senior mission, and she and her husband had to end their mission and come home for extensive, long-term medical care. But they remember their three-month mission with great joy and are thankful they could serve as long as they did.

Have faith in your Heavenly Father and know that He has a missionary plan for you, even though it may not be the plan you had in mind. Instead of serving your mission in Cambodia, you may end up in California. Instead of serving with investigators and converts, you may be using a computer at home to serve those who have passed on and are waiting for your help. What God wants from you is a willing heart and a contrite spirit. He will bless you and your family for generations to come for your faithful service, wherever, and however it is realized.

Summary

- You can serve a mission even if you have disabilities and health problems.
- Senior missionaries are not expected to work as many hours as junior missionaries.
- You should take care of surgeries before you apply for your mission.
- Some medical tests are required before you can serve in a foreign mission.
- Once you decide to serve a mission, begin the hepatitis A and B immunization series.
- You should wait for your call before you get most of your immunization shots.
- You must have health insurance to serve a mission away from home.
- Medicare does not work in foreign countries.
- You will probably need prescriptions from local doctors to obtain medications.

Notes

1. David B. Haight, "Couple Missionaries—'A Wonderful Resource,'" *Ensign*, February 1996.
2. Brenda Frandsen, quoted in Kent D. Watson, "Our Senior Missionaries," *Ensign*, September 2010.

Chapter 7

CLOTHING AND APPEARANCE

The surprising thing most senior missionaries discover when they arrive in the field is that no one really cares how much they weigh, how fashionable they are, or how expensive their clothes are. In fact, being too fashion conscious can actually be a problem. As a missionary, you are often dealing with humble or disadvantaged branch members, converts, and investigators. If you are wearing expensive clothing and jewelry, it makes the people you work with feel threatened and uncomfortable. Besides, expensive clothes are often high maintenance, and you just don't have the time or money to waste on babying clothes. Dozens of things are far more important. Trust me, you will rue the day you bring clothing that has to be dry-cleaned.

Now, this chapter is particularly focused on senior sisters' clothing and appearance. Sisters often have more decisions to make about missionary clothing, cosmetics, and hair concerns than the brethren do. That said, let's take a brief look at some of the issues men will deal with as they decide what to take on their mission.

Especially for Men

It may not be fair, but it's true that men can wear the same suit over and over, and no one will even notice. Besides, people expect male missionaries to look about the same all the time—suit or dark pants, white shirt, and a tie. The only thing they notice is the tie. So male missionaries have lots of fun collecting and trading ties.

Ties

Here's what the Church says about ties:

Wear only business- or professional-style ties. Ties and tiepins should not contain pictures or caricatures. String, bow, skinny, or wide ties are not acceptable. Do not, for any reason, wear ties that draw attention, appear unprofessional, or distract others from your message.[1]

Shirts

Now, about shirts. You are going to *really* hate ironing shirts on your mission. It's worth every penny to get shirts that are wrinkle free, and I mean *wrinkle free*, not wrinkle resistant. Before you buy a shirt, grab a small section of the shirt and squeeze it. If it wrinkles, don't buy it. You will love having crisp, low-maintenance clothing.

You really will want both short- and long-sleeved shirts, so take some of each.

Pants

You don't have to wear a suit all the time. Dark-colored, creased dress pants with a white shirt and tie are totally acceptable and are much more comfortable. Remember, cotton dress pants are far more comfortable than polyester ones in hot, humid climates. And the more wrinkle-resistant your clothing is, the less ironing you will need to do.

Garments

In general, take the kind of garments you are used to. But if you are going to a hot, humid country, take enough to change your garments frequently. Sweaty garments stick to you and make you miserable. Cool showers and fresh garments make a world of difference.

Shoes

Face it. You're going to kill your shoes. Because shoes weigh so much, you will only be able to take a couple of pairs. And buying heavy-duty shoes in other countries is difficult. What you don't want is fancy, leather-soled shoes. You want shoes that will walk happily on cobblestone roads or muddy paths. Your shoes should be comfortable, durable, and easily polished, and they should have thick, heavy-duty soles.

Some tropical missions permit men to wear closed-toe and closed-heel sandals. Your mission will let you know if you need to bring some.

Hair

You'll want to use a short, simple, conservative hairstyle on your mission. You should be able to get an acceptable haircut no matter where you serve. If, however, you are accustomed to coloring your hair, you may need to bring the hair coloring you need with you. Finding specific brands in foreign countries can be challenging, and frequently the postal service is not reliable enough to have items shipped to you.

A Final Note for Men

You're going to be really sorry if you bring clothing that is snug. Many, many senior missionaries gain a bit of weight on their missions, and if you bring tight clothing, you will have to buy new things on your mission. Just be realistic about your weight and the fit of the clothing you bring. Tight pants look terrible and tear easily.

Especially for Women

In a great blog post by Sister Jordyn Hansen, a junior missionary who served in Mexico, she wrote, "Actually I wish I would have packed less. . . . And I wish I wouldn't have bought anything nice or expensive. I don't wear it anyway because I don't want to stand out more, and once you see how you wash it, you realize it's gonna be ruined in a month anyways. So yeah, advice for anyone going to any place like Mexico? Pack only what it says on the list. Seriously."[2]

That said, people are watching you all the time. You represent the Church, so you need to make sure you are always clean, neat, and modest. That means no tight clothes, no short skirts or dresses, no see-through clothes, and no cleavage showing. Tight tops and tight skirts just embarrass everyone around you. In fact, layers work great to cover those pesky bulges anyway.

When the missionary guidelines say to bring conservative clothing, it's not because they want you to look dowdy and feel ugly. They want you to look pretty, feminine, and lovely. What they don't want is for you to attract negative attention or to stand out awkwardly in a crowd. Giant flowers in your hair or bright green nail polish are probably best left at home.

Now, to some extent, your clothing choices will depend on which kind of mission you're called to and where you serve. If you are an MLS missionary, you will be out on the streets and in people's homes a lot, so your clothes will take a real beating. Besides, since many countries, and even many poorer families in the US, don't have air conditioning, you are going to sweat. Take clothing that is simple, basic, easy to care for, and unpretentious. The only time you will dress up a bit is for church.

If you serve in a mission office, you will probably want to dress up a bit more, but not much. Offices often do have air conditioning, so you won't sweat so much. In fact, you'll need a couple of sweaters. Somehow men seem to run hotter than women, and since you may be the only woman in the office, the AC will freeze you to death.

If you serve a public affairs mission, you will be hosting fancy dinners and meeting dignitaries, so you'll have to bump up the level of your clothing. However, you should still go for easy-care, unpretentious outfits.

The Nitty-Gritty about Clothing

Honestly, skirts and blouses will always be your mainstay, even if you always wear dresses at home. One comfortable black skirt can go with dozens of tops and accessories to make a huge variety of outfits. If you add blue, gray, brown, forest green, or red skirts, and you choose your tops and accessories carefully, you've got all the clothing you'll need. It is nice to have a basic black dress, though. You can wear it plain, with a scarf, or add a sweater or jacket to be more formal.

Remember, you don't see the same people every day, so wearing the same clothing fairly often doesn't matter a bit. Yes, you will be sick of those same skirts, and you may want to buy something fun and new while you are on your mission. But taking basic, colorful, easy-care clothing is a really good idea.

As for clothing care, simple is the law of a mission. Many missions don't have clothes dryers. Some don't even have washers. Make sure your clothing is easily washed and is durable. Flimsy tops may be cute, but they will self-destruct in no time at all.

Now, let's talk about some specifics.

Skirts

You almost can't find the kind of skirts you really want in regular stores anymore. Short, straight, tight skirts will make you crazy on a mission. What you want is no-wrinkle, loose, fun skirts. You may have to check out some thrift stores to find suitable ones.

If you are an MLS missionary, having skirts with pockets is heavenly. You will hate carrying a purse around, and besides, purses are easy targets for thieves. It might even be worth it to open a seam in your skirt and just sew a pocket in. If you are domestically challenged, ask a talented friend or relative for help.

If you are going to a humid place, natural fibers are so much better than synthetics. You will end up cursing every polyester skirt you brought. The problem is, polyester sticks to sweaty legs and tangles you up. If you are in an office with air conditioning, artificial fabrics work fine, and they certainly don't wrinkle like cotton does. But in humidity, even cotton blend is less comfortable than pure cotton.

When you choose your skirts, you'll be glad to have a variety of styles. Skirts with cute hemlines, with buttons down the front or side, with fun slash pockets, or with twists and tucks make life fun. But remember, easy-care is the name of the game. You really don't want to have to iron a skirt. If your skirts are cotton, make sure they will hang dry nicely.

Even though basic, one-color skirts will be your staple wardrobe item, having a couple of patterned skirts can be fun. And in warmer, humid climates, colorful, patterned, cotton skirts are the norm for members and missionaries alike. Just make sure you have various tops that will go with each skirt.

Now, this next suggestion is so important that we're reemphasizing it. Leave shortish, tightish skirts at home, even if they are the height of fashion. You will so regret having to constantly tug at your hemline. Comfort is everything when you are working hard in unfamiliar settings. My favorite skirt lengths are somewhere in the calf range: mid-calf, just above, or just below. Skirts that almost hit the floor will make you crazy when you try to work and get around, and they look faddy. Knee-length skirts are best avoided, unless you have really remarkable legs without nylons. Calf-length skirts cover the top of knee-highs (if you really insist on wearing them), and look great with warm socks in the winter, which you actually will wear with pleasure. Besides, calf-length skirts drape beautifully and flatter even old, plump legs. In the winter, you will be glad for longer skirts, (but still not floor-length skirts, which would drag through snow and puddles).

If you bring skirts that just barely fit, chances are very high that you will gain a pound or two and those skirts will no longer be useful—or shouldn't be used, at least. Yes, fashionistas say to stay away from elastic waistbands, but I promise that most of you will love having a flexible waist in your skirts. Besides, tight waists create those awful bulges we all hate.

Tops

Tops don't weigh much, and they create wonderful variety in your wardrobe. Think color. But remember that you represent the Church. You don't want people to stare at the giant fuchsia and turquoise polka dot shirt you thought was so fun, or the rhinestone and sequin kitty decoration you thought was cute.

Patterned tops work great with solid-color skirts, as long as each top can go with more than one skirt. Variety is so fun, and tops will give you variety. Do be aware that plain tops tend to show sweat, so either bring sweat shields (which you can buy in most department stores), or plan to wear lightweight layers. Very lightweight, all-purpose, solid-color, long- and short-sleeved cotton sweaters and jackets are worth their weight in gold.

Also remember, that in humid climates polyester kills for tops, as well as skirts. You will love having loose, feminine, easy-care cotton tops. Clingy tops of any fabric will just make you and everyone around you uncomfortable.

If you can't hang a top to dry and have it look decent, you will regret bringing it. Ironing tiny pleats or ruffles will be beyond irritating. Simple, colorful, flattering tops will help you feel pretty even when you have been out on the street or in the office for hours.

Avoid see-through tops (even the sleeves) and tops that barely cover your garments. You will regret bringing them.

Dresses

Having a couple of dresses that go with several jackets or sweaters is a fun change from skirts, skirts, and more skirts. However, I have found that dresses are mostly for church or other more formal situations. You may need more dresses if you are serving in public relations or in an area office, where the dress standards are more formal.

The same cautions apply to dresses as to skirts and tops—keep them feminine, conservative, and easy to care for. Avoid see-through portions, spangles, over-the-top patterns, and anything too tight, too low-cut, or too short. Unlike skirts, dresses get much shorter when you sit in them or when you bend over, so buy them mid-calf length.

Sweaters and Jackets

These two items are severely underrated, especially sweaters. You will love having a yellow or periwinkle cardigan to brighten up your skirt and blouse outfit. Short- or long-sleeved, sweaters create layers and cover tummies. You will want to bring several. Just make sure they aren't too tight. A tight sweater over a blouse irritates your underarms and doesn't mask your tummy.

Generally, you are going to like lightweight sweaters far more than heavy ones, unless you're working outdoors in a cold country. Then you'll want to wear a warm sweater under a warm coat. You'll want to wear lightweight sweaters in air-conditioned buildings and in the spring and fall. Even in the winter, a lightweight sweater fits comfortably under a coat. If you have a sweater that matches each of your skirts, you'll have a ready-made suit and a huge increase in the number and variety of available outfits.

Jackets work the same way. If your jacket is too heavy, it will constrict your arms while you try to work. Jackets are nice though, for dressier situations like church or more formal dinners. A pretty, colorful jacket can really perk up a boring shirt, and when you add accessories, you'll look top-notch. Sister missionaries often take too many jackets and too few sweaters. Jackets have limited use in real-life missionary work.

Underwear

Slips

Surprisingly enough, many countries do not know what a slip is, so bring a dark slip and a white slip with you. If you are wearing light-colored, cotton skirts, you will be embarrassed if people can see through your skirt. Clearly, adding a slip, especially a slip that is made of nylon or another synthetic fabric, will wipe out the benefit of having a cotton skirt, so, ideally, you should bring a very lightweight cotton slip or buy skirts that have their own lining.

Bras

You don't need very many bras, but having a dark one and a light one is a good idea. Sometimes white bras show through dark tops and look really tacky. And of course, dark bras under light tops are even worse.

Temple Garments

If you're going to a humid climate, you will need more temple garments than other missionaries because you will want to change them more often. Sweaty garments that stick to you and your clothes are really uncomfortable. There is a great deal of disagreement on which garment fabric works best in humidity. Many sisters still like silky garments and find that mesh or cotton ones are not all that comfortable. However, you should spend the money and try a mesh or cotton top before you buy a bunch of them. Try exercising in them or going for a strenuous walk. The tighter, stretchy garments will probably make you miserable in a humid country, even if they're really popular right now.

Remember, garments are made to be a guideline for your clothing choices. You will really hate constantly tugging at a neckline, hem, or sleeve because your garments are showing. And it is always awkward to see a sister cross her legs and show her underwear.

Stockings

Sister missionaries are no longer required to wear nylon stockings, and most of us are thrilled. If you do choose to wear knee-high stockings, please, please sit in front of a mirror and see if the top of your stockings show when you cross your legs. If they do, buy a longer skirt and try again or skip the knee-high stockings altogether. Tugging a skirt down over and over to cover knee-high nylons doesn't really work.

Tights, however, are still frequently worn and look nice. They are especially great in cold climates. In fact, you may find yourself wearing tights, leggings, and long socks under your skirts during the cold, humid winters in some countries. One senior sister was so worried about having cold feet that she brought a pair of battery-powered socks from a sports equipment store, but then, in the country where she served the D batteries cost $3 a piece and only lasted a couple of hours. So, the socks stayed in her suitcase. Layers of socks are probably more practical.

Wearing leggings that don't cover your feet is too casual for a missionary, but if you wear knee-high socks on top of them, you're fine. By the way, a skirt above your knees is still too short, even if you're wearing tights or leggings under it. Remember, as a missionary, you represent the Church, and fashion is not your primary goal.

Accessories

Having a number of scarves, belts, necklaces, and earrings can really perk up your outfits. Think of the difference between a plain black skirt with a plain pink top and those same clothes with a fun necklace or scarf added. The nice thing is that scarves and jewelry use up very little space and weight in your bags. But don't bring expensive jewelry or accessories. They are just begging to get stolen. In fact, many senior sisters leave their diamond wedding rings at home and just wear a simple band or a CTR ring.

You can have fun jewelry without going over the top. You don't need earrings that blow in the wind or hit your shoulders. You don't need necklaces that are so big and heavy that they hurt your neck. Bring fun accessories, but don't go wild. You can be conservative and still feel cute. Obviously, it is a good idea to bring accessories that will go with many different outfits.

Shoes

Can you imagine walking in heels on cobblestones? Trust me, it's almost impossible. How about suede or good leather shoes during a rainstorm on flooded streets? Your shoes are going to be your best friend if you are serving a mission that takes you outside. Even inside, you'll be very glad to have pain-free feet. It is so difficult to be totally practical with shoes, especially when you love them and are used to having a dozen or more pairs.

Unfortunately, shoes take a lot of luggage space and are quite heavy, so fewer is better. That means that the few shoes you do take should be very carefully chosen. Oddly enough, since you are always wearing a black missionary tag, wearing black shoes looks very nice. Thick, padded soles and insoles are essential if you're walking much at all. Flat is fabulous. Plenty of toe room is vital, so those lovely pointed toes probably won't work for a mission. A strap across your arch will keep your shoes on your feet without stress. Plastic shoes can make your feet sweat in humid countries, but they are great in a rainstorm. Sandals are allowed all over the world now, but you'll be happier if your sandals will stand up to a serious walking. Of course flip-flops, even cute ones with flowers and rhinestones, are not going to be allowed outside your apartment. If you ignore me and bring heels or thin strappy sandals, they will enjoy a wonderful mission in the back of your closet.

You'll want to shop around and check the Internet for your shoe options. You can find practical shoes that are still attractive and make you feel pretty. However, good shoes are not cheap. Do not take shoes you haven't tested, or your favorite shoes that you think you can't live without unless they are also comfortable and durable.

Hair

You're going to fuss about this a bit, but the reality is, that on a mission your hair can be a real pain. That great razor cut you love so much may have to be something you come home to. Work with your beautician to find a cut that can be replicated by a normal, friendly, foreign hairdresser. The texture and quality of hair in other countries is very different from American hair. They often have thicker, coarser hair; so foreign beauticians may have no idea how to handle our fine, thin, old-lady hair.

After you arrive in your mission, your great pre-mission haircut will disappear. Be patient. Look around you as you shop or walk. If you see someone with a haircut you think will work for you, ask them who cuts their hair. Beware, though. Just because their cut looks great doesn't mean yours will. If you do get a bad cut, take comfort in the mantra, "No one but me really cares how I look, anyway." And luckily, your hair will grow out.

Stay away from radical, shaved, dramatic styles that make you the center of attention instead of your message. Simple, humble members will not really love your crazy hairstyle, and it will distance you from them.

What you want is a wash-and-wear style. You just don't have the time or energy to mess with your hair for half an hour. You want something you can wash, add whatever goop you love, blow dry, tease or use a curling iron here and there, spray, and be good to go.

Now, for color. Many of us are not quite ready to go gray. However, if you do have gray hair, you're lucky! No fuss. But if you choose to color your hair, do it regularly! An inch of gray roots looks really, really bad if your hair is dark. Blondes can get away with less attention to their roots. You can get your hair colored in most countries, but you may or may not like the way it comes out. Streaking and weaving are pretty expensive, if they are available at all. As with haircuts, don't get too frantic about your hair as you experiment. Your hair will grow.

Your best bet is to experiment before your mission with coloring your own hair, if you dare. The key is to use a shade lighter than your natural color. And then put the coloring only on your gray roots for about forty-five or fifty minutes. Then put the remaining color—no, you can't put the whole bottle on your roots—on the rest of your hair, spread it evenly through your hair, and leave it for ten minutes. You can do it! Some sisters bring their favorite coloring from home, but you'll need a new bottle every six weeks or two months. Sisters with short hair can divide one bottle into two applications. If you're planning to have hair color mailed to you, be aware that many countries have less-than-reliable postal systems. In those countries, it's best to bring hair color for your whole mission with you.

And perms. If you can wean yourself away from a perm, you will probably be happier on your mission, but if not, you can get perms most places. They are time-consuming and expensive and may come out different than you expected. But if you can do a wash-and-wear style with your perm, it will be well worth the time and effort.

Now, for hair products. With very few exceptions, hair products simply weigh too much to bring with you. Just bring travel sizes so you can get by until you can get to a store. You can usually buy shampoo, mousse, hairspray, and gel wherever you are assigned. The exceptions you may want to consider are hair color products and small specialty styling products.

Makeup

You don't have to give up your makeup when you go on a mission, but you may want to use less of it. If you're used to wearing lots of dark, dramatic eye shadow, for example, you may want to tone it down. But using foundation, blush, mascara, eyeliner, brow pencil, and conservative lipstick is pretty normal anywhere in the world.

The bigger key, though, is to get long-lasting makeup. Sweat is really hard on makeup. Some of the new twenty-four-hour makeup really does last longer, even though it doesn't last for twenty-four hours.

You would be very wise to test how long a tube of mascara or lipstick lasts you, if you use it every day. Otherwise you won't know how many tubes you will need for your mission. You can buy some brands of makeup in some countries, but all cosmetics are about twice as expensive in foreign countries as they are in the States. If you're willing to pay double, use the computer to see if a brand you love is sold in your mission field. Remember, don't rely on foreign postal services—even, or perhaps especially, when you order something online.

Nails

You can get manicures all over the world. However, maintaining artificial nails is expensive and time-consuming. You may want to think twice about keeping your fake nails. However, if you must have artificial nails, keep them relatively short. One sister brought her own nail supplies and just had a local manicurist apply it.

When you're talking to an investigator, you really don't want their attention on your fingers because your polish is so bright and fascinating. Fingernail polish is fun, but if you choose to use it, keep it subtle and well-maintained.

Many, many senior sisters paint their toenails when they are wearing sandals. It's a fun way to baby yourself, as long as you use a fairly moderate color. However, some of us can't reach our toes, so coloring our toenails is not a real option.

Casual Clothes

Over and over, sisters moan that they didn't bring enough casual clothes. Whether you hang around the apartment in the mornings because you run a youth center at night, or you hang around the apartment at night because you work in a mission office during the day, there are going to be several hours a day—and many hours on P-day—that you will want comfortable, casual clothes to wear. Some sisters wear loose dresses, and some wear pants. Whichever you choose, bring enough to give you some variety. One pair of pants is simply not enough for a whole mission. Make sure your casual clothes are comfortable. When you want to relax, you want relaxed clothes too.

Summary

Men

- Cotton shirts and pants are more comfortable in humid climates.
- Bring wrinkle-free shirts.
- Ties should be professional and conservative.
- Shoes should be heavy-duty and absolutely must have thick, long-lasting soles.
- Use a short, conservative, and easy to maintain hairstyle.
- Bring clothes that will handle the few extra pounds you may gain.

Women

- Choose easy-care, wash-and-wear, fun, feminine clothes.
- Avoid clothes that are too tight, too short, too sheer, too loud, or too expensive.
- Accessories will keep you smiling. Bring inexpensive scarves and jewelry.
- Choose a very few practical, low-heeled, thick-soled shoes (that are still cute!).
- Experiment with a moderate, wash-and-wear hairstyle that can be easily maintained.
- Subdued, long-lasting makeup will make you feel pretty, so bring enough for your whole mission. Don't count on getting things shipped to you.

Notes

1. missionary.lds.org/clothing/elder/guidelines?lang=eng.
2. Jordyn Hansen, "Nothing is a Coincidence," *Caminando en Chiapas*, hermanahansenmexico.blogspot.com.

Chapter 8

ALL THINGS ELECTRICAL
AND ELECTRONIC

But as a senior missionary, can I call my kids and grandkids more than twice a year?" you may ask, panicking. "And will my cell phone even work in a foreign country?" Fear not. There are many good ways to keep in contact with your family while you are serving a mission. You will be able to talk to your family and friends frequently. There are even ways to make your home phone work in a different state or country.

It's important for you to understand that senior missionaries have different schedules and rules than junior missionaries. There is absolutely no way you can be on task sixteen hours a day. Many of us can't even work eight hours a day. So, realistically, you are going to have some downtime—time when you must rest, but you don't need to sleep. In this downtime, you are allowed to read novels that are not religious, listen to nonreligious music, search the web, and even watch movies. Media, however, can be uplifting or destructive, so you must take care to feed your soul with the media you choose, whether it be books, movies, or music.

Now much of your downtime may involve electronics and electricity, so let's look at some details. Communicating with your family is really important during your mission, so before we talk about electricity, let's talk about phones, since they matter more to you than voltage and electrical outlets. Just remember that your phones won't work if you don't have the correct adaptors and outlets, which we will also discuss in this chapter. (See also Appendixes B and C.)

Cell, Smart, and VoIP Phones

Before you make any decisions about taking your cell phone on your mission, check with your mission office. Many, but not all, missions provide cell phones for their missionaries, and those cell phones will use a local provider. If you use your US cell phone in a foreign country, you may be charged roaming charges for each call you make, whereas a local phone will have no extra charges. In some countries, however, you are charged for every minute you use your local phone.

If your mission does not provide a cell phone, you can get a local pay-as-you-go contract with a cell phone provider in your mission country. This kind of contract only charges for the actual minutes you use. In developing countries, people are often charged for each minute on calls they make, but they are not charged for calls they receive. As a result, if someone needs to contact you, they will call you and ask you to call them right back. That way, they are only charged for a minute or two, and you, who probably has more money than they do, pay for most of the call. And that's okay.

Now, what about smartphones? As long as you use your smartphone as a mini computer and not as a phone, you may be glad to have it on your mission. You can use many apps without an Internet connection, and you can use the Internet when you have Wi-Fi available. Just make sure that you are using a secure Wi-Fi connection. Airport and fast food restaurant Wi-Fi connections are easily hacked.

If you want to call your family, remember to use this privilege wisely. There are no rules about how often or how long you can talk, but you are on a mission, and talking to your family and friends should not interfere with your missionary work.

You can virtually attend family functions using Skype, FaceTime, or other applications. It's wonderful to be able to see a new grandbaby or talk to a grandchild face-to-face on their birthday. We've even carried our laptop from room to room to give our children a tour of our mission apartment. It's so nice to physically see that everyone is still healthy and happy—or not, as the case may be.

Many senior missionary couples bring their home phones with them and use them on their missions outside the borders of the US by using VoIP (Voice over Internet Protocol). You may have heard of Vonage, magicJack, or Google Voice; there are other services available too. Some of these products require a monthly or yearly fee and/or a charge for the device that hooks into your computer, but others are free or very inexpensive. Some services can use your home phone number too. Do a comparative search on the Internet to see what your options are.

If you decide to use a VoIP system, you don't need to take your actual phone to your mission, just the connecting device that accesses your home phone number. Often there will already be a phone in your apartment that you can attach to the VoIP device you bring with you. We used a VoIP phone on our last mission, and it was wonderful to be able to call our US bank or insurance company or doctor or relative whenever we wanted to, all handled as a local US call. The clarity of the calls was so good you'd swear you were calling from home. But remember, you need to set up your VoIP system *before* you leave on your mission so you can bring the device with you that makes your phone calls possible.

Computers

Now, let's talk a bit about computers, since you may be using a computer to make phone calls and lots and lots of other things. You can watch movies on your computer; you can read books on your computer; you can talk to your family face-to-face on your computer; you can send emails and pay bills on your computer; and you can research health questions, cultural conundrums, and a zillion other things on your computer. That's why we were *so* glad we brought *two* laptops with us. Having two laptops saves lots of couples tension over who gets to use the computer when and for how long. Besides, if one of your laptops breaks or is stolen, you still have a computer available. Buying computers in developing countries is expensive, and they might not work when you return to the US because the plugs are different.

Most apartments for senior missionaries will not have a desktop computer included, and you'll need to check with your mission office to see if the apartment they have for you has Internet included. If not, when you get to your mission, you will need to get an Internet service with a local company. Be aware that the Internet in developing countries can be very, very slow, making it difficult to stream movies or even to video chat. However, it's still vital to have access to the Internet as a senior missionary, so be patient with the slower system. On one of our missions, we purchased a little thumb-sized device that plugged right into a USB port and gave us Internet access wherever we took our computer, which was very convenient indeed. You may be required to sign a contract for Internet service, so you need to make sure the contract ends when your mission does and that it is all paid for before you leave your mission.

Some of you may want to bring a movie streaming system like Roku or Netflix with you for movie watching. We didn't bring anything like that, but our friends who did were not very satisfied. Most local broadband systems are just not capable of handling the demands of movie streaming. Besides, having that kind of access to movies may be a serious temptation to those of us who are used to spacing out in front of the TV.

E-Books from Your Local Library

Before you leave, you should check with your local library to see if you can access e-books with your library card. It can be very difficult to find books in English if you are serving in another country. And even if you're serving in the US, having access to thousands of books on your computer or smartphone is wonderful.

If your local library offers online e-books, the librarians can direct you to the online library system, which will have links to the e-book system and online book reader apps. Get everything working before you leave, and test it while you can still get help from your local librarian. It's really, really hard to try to set up the system from a foreign country. I used my online library, and the e-books I could check out constantly. I only wished I could put more than five e-books on hold at a time, since some popular ones took more than a month or two to be available.

Electronic Devices and Electrical Appliances

Getting any electrical device to work in another country can be challenging. Most modern electronic devices like computers, laptops, smartphones, cameras, and CPAP machines are dual-voltage capable. That means that they will work in countries that use 110 V systems (like the US), and countries that use 220 V systems (like most other countries). Check on the Internet (or in Appendix B) to see what voltage your mission country uses.

For dual voltage devices, you will still need to get electrical adaptors for the plugs, so that you can plug them into the outlets designed for that specific country. Check on the Internet (or in Appendix B) to see what kind of plug you will need for your mission. The US, as you know, uses two flat vertical projections for their plugs. Some countries use two round plug projections, some use two large diagonal projections, some use three rectangular projections, and some use three round projections. Of course, their outlets correlate with the type of plug the country uses. That's why you may need adaptors for your electronic devices.

You can buy adaptors before you leave for your mission, but be aware that many senior couple apartments have been used previously by couples who have chosen to leave their adaptors in the apartment. If you do need more adaptors, they are *much cheaper* in your mission country than they are in the US. But it's a good idea to bring one or two with you so you can plug your computer in right away.

Most electrical appliances do not have dual voltage, so if you plug them into a 220 V socket, not only will they not work, but the appliance will burn out and be ruined. You can buy adaptors that are also transformers, changing the device so it will work with 220 V, but these transformers don't work for any appliance that has variable speeds, such as a blender, or an appliance that uses heat, such as a hairdryer or curling iron. For some reason, electric alarm clocks and razors don't work well with transformers either. However, if you check carefully, you may be able to buy dual-voltage appliances. These appliances have a switch on them that can change the appliance from 110 V to 220 V.

Voltage is not the only issue on appliances, however. Alternating electric current alternates at 60 cycles per second in the US, but at 50 cycles or at some other rate in other countries. (See Appendix B.) Your appliances are designed to work with the frequency used in your country, and usually on the device label it will say something like "60Hz," which means it is designed to operate at a frequency of 60 cycles per second. If you plug your appliance in to a system that uses a different frequency, it will burn out the device, and transformers will not necessarily prevent that problem.

That's why it's smarter to just wait until you get to your mission to buy small appliances, and transformers are expensive and heavy. Besides, your apartment should be supplied with many small appliances such as toasters and blenders. Sometimes previous missionaries have left behind 220 V hairdryers, hair clippers, and alarm clocks, since 220 V appliances won't work in the US.

We talk about packing in chapter 9, but as you pack, you're going to find that you have *way* less room and weight allowance than you thought you needed. So not taking appliances and transformers will really save you space and weight.

Your mission office will be able to answer mission-specific questions you have about electronics and electrical devices. Just email them *before* you buy things for your mission so you won't waste money on items that won't work or are already provided by the mission.

DVDs

You may want to be aware that DVDs you bring with you from the US won't work in the DVD players that are already in your apartment, or that you decide to purchase there. Somehow they format them differently in different parts of the world. So, if you buy DVDs on your mission, you might as well leave them there when you go home. But if your laptop will play DVDs, you'll want to bring the ones you want to watch on it with you.

Music

Music can be a very important tool to help you relax and to lift your spirits. But your choice of music may not be your spouse's preference. You will be lots happier if you bring a set of good, comfortable headphones to use with your computer, so that whatever media you or your spouse are accessing does not have to be broadcast throughout the apartment.

You will also find it very useful to have CDs of Church music, especially Primary and youth music, since your mission ward or branch may not know how those songs are actually supposed to sound. If you've never heard the newest Primary program song or a young women's song, trying to figure out the melody can be frustrating. Being able to sing along to a recording is a lifesaver.

And remember, it's perfectly acceptable to listen to nonreligious music, but as with all media, you should be sensitive to the Spirit and make sure to feed your soul.

Summary

- Don't bring your cell phone.
- Smartphones are okay, but not for phone calls.
- Set up a VoIP phone system before you leave.
- Bring two laptop computers.
- Don't bring a video streaming system.
- Set up an e-book check-out system with your local library.
- Don't bring electrical appliances unless they are dual-voltage.
- Don't bring transformers; only bring a couple of adaptors.
- Don't bring DVDs unless your laptop will play them.
- Focus on uplifting media.
- Bring two sets of good, comfortable headphones.
- Bring recordings of Primary and youth program songs.

Chapter 9

A WHOLE MISSION IN TWO SUITCASES—ARE YOU KIDDING?

When deciding what and what not to bring with you on your mission, much depends on where you are serving. If you are serving stateside, you will be able to bring a car, which you can load with almost anything you want. However, if you are flying to your mission, the limitations on luggage are drastic. It will seem impossible to fit everything you need and want to have on your mission in just two suitcases and a carry-on bag, but it can be done. You just have to plan carefully, and pack even more carefully.

Because you are a senior missionary, you will probably be assigned to one apartment for your entire mission, and that apartment will be furnished not only with furniture, but also with basic supplies.

Frequently, the apartment you are assigned to will have been previously used by one or more senior couples, so when you arrive, you may be shocked to find that your apartment is not empty like a commercial furnished apartment would be. There will be all kinds of treasures there that other couples thought you might love to have. There may be adaptors and transformers, office supplies, and sewing supplies. There may be hair clippers and hairdryers, hand mirrors, and a bathroom scale. You may even find insect repellant, first aid supplies, shampoo, hand lotion, and vitamins. But, you may also be dismayed to find unopened, expired packages of food that someone thought you could use.

We loved all the treasures we found, but we know some couples who just loaded them all up and tossed them out or made them available to other couples in the area. Be patient. The senior couples who left those treasures only left things they thought you would love to have, like special cooking tools or hard-to-find spices. The supplies you find in your apartment will probably save you a great deal of money, but even more important, they will save you packing space. However, if you are getting a new apartment that previous couples haven't supplied, you may need to think twice about the Dos and Don'ts of packing listed below.

Dos and Don'ts of Packing

- One of the things you almost surely *do not* want to bring with you, even though they will be listed to bring, is books. In your apartment, you will likely find copies of the scriptures and *Preach My Gospel*, as well as many other Church books. Books are just too heavy to bring, and you can load dozens of books onto your smartphone, iPad, e-reader, or computer.
- You also do not want to bring anything bulky or heavy that you can easily buy in your mission location. Don't bring an electric clock. Don't bring an umbrella. Don't bring cute things to decorate with. Don't bring heavy boots for cold weather or a heavy winter coat, and if you must bring heavy clothing items, wear them onto the plane instead of packing them. Unlike

junior missionaries, you will not be outside all day in bad weather. You can frequently purchase clothing better suited to your mission climate after you arrive there. Many senior missionaries never use their heavy-duty lined raincoats at all. Check with your mission office before you buy expensive, heavy clothing. (See chapter 7 for specific information on clothing and makeup.)

- Now, your apartment will have sheets and towels. They will probably not be new, though, so if that matters to you, you will want to consider buying them after you see what's available. Do check with your mission office before you leave home to find out how difficult it is to purchase good sheets and towels if you decide to go that route. Taking linens in your limited luggage is almost prohibitive.

- Do bring small containers of shampoo, conditioner, shaving cream, toothpaste, and any other supplies to get you by while you're in the MTC and during the first week or so of your mission.

- Do bring supplements you may not be able to find in your new country. For example, some countries do not sell melatonin, which some of us use to get to sleep. Some don't have vitamin D3 or B complex vitamins. Many seniors simply take a good multivitamin and mineral tablet every day on their missions and that is sufficient. If it isn't sufficient for you, check with your mission office and research on the Internet to see what vitamins, minerals, and supplements are available in your country.

- Do bring prescription medications with you to get you started. You probably won't be able to bring enough for your whole mission, though, and

bringing prescriptions from home won't work in
other countries. You'll have to get a local doctor to
write your prescriptions, especially if you are taking
controlled substances such as Ritalin or Adderall.

- If you use a CPAP machine, you will be able to take
it on the plane in its own small case, and it will not
count as a bag. Check with your mission office to
see if CPAP supplies are available in your mission.
All medical supplies can be taken on planes without
counting against your luggage limit. I even took a
large portable backrest with me on the plane, so I
could survive the long flight and bad office chairs
on both my missions. I also took blow-up cushions
to help me endure hard armrests and bad airplane
seats. You do need to advise the airline that you have
medical supplies so that they can put a tag on those
items.

- Do bring pictures of your family to enjoy and to show
members and investigators, but don't bring the frames.
Do bring a copy of your patriarchal blessing, perhaps
online. Do bring your journal, either a hard copy or
online, and do write in it regularly. Do bring a vial
of consecrated oil. Do bring a bunch of your favorite
recipes. You will be cooking *a lot* for yourselves, for
missionaries, and for members and investigators. You
may want to type up your recipes or scan them onto
your computer to save space.

- Don't bring measuring cups and spoons, even if
your new country uses metric measuring. Previous
couples will likely have left US measuring devices
in your apartment. These measuring devices are
really essential to make your recipes work, though,
so ask your mission office if you need them. Since

my husband loves to bake pies, he brought a pastry cutter on our last mission. Most foreign cooks don't make American-style pies, so you can't buy the pastry cutters.

- If you're noise sensitive, apartment living (especially with no air conditioning and your windows wide open), can be *very* noisy. Do bring white noise to help you sleep through the party next door or the music outside. You can download white noise on your smartphone or computer, or you can purchase a separate white-noise machine. Do test the white noise before you leave to make sure it will work for you.
- Don't bring too many shoes. They are heavy and take up a lot of luggage space. Wear your heaviest shoes on the plane, and pack your jewelry, makeup, and any other small items inside your other two or three pairs of shoes.
- Don't bring hangers. Previous couples will have left some in your apartment. If you need more, you can buy them inexpensively from a dry-cleaning shop.

Packing Hints

The Missionary Travel Office documents will tell you how many bags and what sized bags you are allowed to take to your mission. Generally, you will be allowed two large bags that can weigh no more than fifty pounds each (including the bag), and one carry-on bag of limited dimensions that can only weigh thirty-five to forty pounds (including the bag). However, some airlines will only allow one free bag, and some limit carry-on bag weight to as few as twelve pounds. If you have to switch airlines on the way to your mission, you will have to follow the limitations of the most restrictive airline.

That said, your mission will frequently pay for the luggage charges needed to permit you to bring two large bags and one regular carry-on bag. If you have to pay excess weight charges to be able to take the fifty pounds per bag you should be allowed, keep your receipt so you can be reimbursed by your mission.

You will also be allowed to bring one personal bag, such as a computer case or a purse. But airlines are getting more and more picky about your personal bag. They often have size and weight restrictions for these bags too. If an airline does give you trouble about your personal bag, just put some things in your pockets or your carry-on bag or your spouse's bag, and stay calm.

Remember to follow TSA security requirements. Go to www.tsa.gov and click the "Travel" tab, and then select "Security Screening" from the drop-down menu to find all the details on what is allowed and what isn't. No, you can't carry a knife to peel the orange you plan to carry in your personal bag. No, you can't take your favorite multi-tool either. If you bring these items they will be taken away from you at the airport, and you probably won't ever get them back. You can't even bring a container of yogurt or a full bottle of water. Any liquids you want to take on the plane must fit in three-ounce containers, and all the containers must fit in one quart-sized, see-through bag.

You can pack all the liquids and sharp things you want in your checked bag, but remember that liquids are heavy.

Bags

Unfortunately, almost all empty bags weigh more than ten pounds per bag. When you only get fifty pounds total, giving up ten of those pounds for the bag itself is just not fair. Junior missionaries have to have really strong bags because they are moving every couple of months. You, however, are usually only using your bags to get to your mission and to get back home.

So, we didn't take heavy, expensive bags. Instead we took nylon duffel bags with wheels because they only weighed four or five pounds. These bags aren't really made to handle fifty pounds, though, so you may need to belt them around for extra support or strategically wrap duct tape around them, leaving space for the zipper to be opened if the bag needs to be inspected. If you can't deal with taking weird-looking luggage, just take the lightest bags you can find.

The disadvantage of using a duffel bag is that it has to be pulled by a band at the top, so the bag is unwieldy and difficult to manage in airports. The solution is to rent a luggage cart as soon as you possibly can at the airport. In fact, because you will each be wearing your heaviest clothing, dragging two very heavy bags, and trying to add a heavy carry-on bag and a personal bag, plus any medical supplies you are bringing, you're going to need that luggage cart, and extra help too. Just pay the fees for a luggage cart and a porter. It's worth the money.

Packing

I have found that by using vacuum packing bags—the kind that you fill and then suck or roll out all the air—I can fit lots of clothing items in two large bags. The problem is that even if you take out all the air, the clothes still weigh the same amount. So weight becomes the real packing monster.

Try to select lightweight clothes, if at all possible. Leave your heavy sweaters, skirts, and shoes at home, unless you can wear them on the plane. Plan to use layers to stay warm instead. Tops weigh less than skirts, so bring more of them to create many more outfits. Cardigans and washable, light-weight jackets are lighter than blazers and suits, so bring more of them.

Take things like makeup and hair coloring supplies out of their packaging to save space and weight. You can put them in small ziplock bags to keep things organized. Put vitamins and supplements in labeled ziplock bags too. But, leave prescriptions in their original packages, since baggage inspectors are more cautious about prescription drugs.

Remember, everything (but the quart-sized bag of liquids, filled with no more than three-ounce-sized containers) that you can't bring in your carry-on bag must go in your checked bags, and liquids are heavy, so avoid bringing them if you possibly can. You can buy local brands in your mission that will probably be sufficient.

I try to put my heaviest things in my carry-on bag, even though that makes it difficult to drag through the airport. Your carry-on bag is smaller, but you are still allowed thirty to forty pounds in it. So smaller, heavier thing like books (if you insist), pills, supplements, and other heavy non-liquids—even shoes—are good, but use your space most efficiently.

In your personal bag, put things you will need to use as you travel. For me, that means protein bars, cheese, other food, pills, reading material, my computer, an e-reader, and blow-up pillows. For you, it may mean something completely different. Personal bags are easily stolen, so keep a careful watch on them.

You should always be especially careful with your passport, driver's license, and money when you travel. My husband and I usually carry them in a small cloth envelope on a cord around our necks. You can buy these envelopes in the travel section at many stores. Putting valuable documents in a purse or briefcase is just too risky, since airports are prime spots for thieves.

Weighing In

A couple of days before you are scheduled to leave for your mission, do a trial packing. Get everything you plan to take, and that means every single little thing, and practice packing it. See how it will all fit most efficiently. Decide what you can really do without. Put everything in the container or baggie you plan to take it in. Make sure you have your toothbrush and razor. Get all your documents together. Pretend like you are leaving the next morning.

Then, put your bathroom scale on a hard floor that has lots of space. Weigh yourself first and write down the number. You can keep your shoes on when you weigh yourself, because, for once, what you weigh doesn't matter a bit. It's just a baseline number so that you can weigh your luggage. Then step off the scale, let it zero again, and step back on while holding one suitcase. Subtract your weight from the new weight, and voilà, you have the weight of your suitcase.

You can also purchase a gizmo that you can hang your bag on and it will tell you what that bag weighs. But why miss out on the chance to make a fabulous memory jumping on and off the scale?

Now, chances are someone's bags will be overweight and the other's will be underweight. Never fear. Just shift things around and balance out the space. There's no rule that each bag must contain only one spouse's possessions.

Summary

- The apartments provided for senior couples are furnished and have lots of supplies. Check with your mission office to see what you will have available and what can be purchased locally.

- You only get two large suitcases that weigh up to fifty pounds each, one carry-on that often can weigh thirty to forty pounds, and one personal bag of limited size and weight.
- Choose lightweight luggage.
- Use vacuum packing bags to fit more items in a suitcase.
- Bring only enough personal care items, such as shampoo, to last you through the MTC and the first week in your mission. Buy the rest in your mission.
- Bring items that are lightweight.
- Wear your heaviest shoes and coats on the airplane.
- Take things out of their packaging to save weight and space.
- Keep prescriptions in their original containers.
- Put heavier items in your carry-on bag.
- Guard your personal bag and keep it in your sight.
- Put your passport and money in a neck wallet, but keep it accessible, since you will need your passport at the airport.
- A few days before you leave for your mission, pack all your bags and weigh them.

Chapter 10

GETTING THERE

The Church's missionary travel website has general travel information, including information on visas and passports. Although the information is geared toward junior missionaries and their parents, you will find answers to some of your questions there too.[1]

Driving

If you are serving a mission in the United States or Canada, you will probably be able to drive your personal car to your mission. In that case, instead of having to pack what seems like all your worldly possessions into two suitcases, you will have one big automobile available to pack. However, you will be amazed at how quickly a trunk and backseat can fill up, so plan carefully. What you learned in chapter 9 about packing can also be applied to packing your car. Many of the things you think are essential will already be in your apartment or can be purchased after you arrive.

For some missions in Church recreational sites and historic sites, you may be required to bring an RV to live in during your mission. In that case, you will need to bring all the household living supplies that are usually provided in a senior couple apartment, but you will have lots more space to pack them in. You may be required to pay a monthly RV parking pad fee. Check with your mission.

The MTC provides secure parking for your car or RV, so you can safely pack your valuables in your vehicle. Then, when your MTC experience ends, you can simply drive to your mission. Do make sure your car or RV is tuned up and ready for a long trip. Check your tires too. You want your trip to be fun and problem-free.

Flying

The Airport

Some of you have flown a lot, so you know all about security requirements and airports. But for those of you who are newbies to flying or have never traveled outside the US, let's talk about what to expect as you travel to your mission.

The Missionary Travel Office has agreements set up with various airlines to minimize the cost of missionary travel. They also have to set up flights for thousands of missionaries who are traveling all over the world. So, they don't really deal with personal preferences and convenient flight schedules. They are focused on getting you to your mission on time and inexpensively.

As a result, your mission travel experience can be challenging. Frequently, your mission trip will start very early in the morning, since you need to be at the airport two or three hours early for international flights. If you are using MTC transportation to get to the airport, you may be included in a group of junior missionaries who are also flying out that day, some on flights that may leave long before yours. Consequently, you may have to get to the airport several hours before you would normally need to be there. So, if you have family or friends who can pick you up from the MTC or your home and take you to the airport, you can control your schedule a bit better.

When you get to the airport, you will be tired from having to get up early. Do get help lugging your many heavy bags inside the airport and to your airline's check-in counter. You may be surprised to find that you have been scheduled a return flight that you knew nothing about. This flight is necessary for various countries' visa requirements, but you can just ignore it. At the counter, they will check-in your big, heavy checked bags and send them directly to your final destination, your mission city, even though you may have one or more flight layovers on the way.

To review TSA requirements, go to www.tsa.gov. Usually the things airport security makes you throw away are things you carry without thinking about them—small things in your purse or pockets or on your keychain.

Once you get to your assigned boarding gate, you may want to make sure that your medical supplies, such as your CPAP machine, are given a label so that they won't count as carry-on luggage.

The Flight

If going international, your flight will probably begin with a one- to four-hour flight to a US city, and that flight may be on a smaller plane. Before you board your long international flight, you will have a layover in a US airport. That layover can be short or it can last for many, many hours, and you will already be tired. So try to find a quiet place to rest.

No matter how well you prepare, your long international flight will be an endurance experience. But here are some things you can do to make it easier.

1. Bring a neck cushion that you can lean your head against to sleep.
2. Bring a sweater to wear during your flight. Airplanes are notoriously cold, especially during overnight flights.
3. Drink water and try to get up and move around every hour or so to avoid getting blood clots in your legs.
4. Some people bring sanitary wipes to use on their armrests and pull-down tray.
5. Earplugs, eye covers, and white noise or calm music will help you sleep during your flight. Airplanes are noisy, bright, and busy.
6. Frequently, airlines do not provide movies unless you pay for them. Bring your own movies, e-books, or projects to work on. TSA allows sewing needles, small scissors, knitting needles, and crochet hooks, so don't worry about bringing some hand work.

After You Arrive

Someone from your mission will be at the airport to help you collect your bags and take you to the mission home or office. There you will meet your mission president and his wife. They will know that you are exhausted from your flight because they will have made that trip more than once themselves. They will feed you and give you a room in the mission home, or someone will take you to your apartment to settle in and sleep.

One funny story, though. When we arrived in Portugal, after more than twenty hours in transit, we were just exhausted.

Our wonderful mission president and his wife decided to give us our assigned phone and a car with GPS and lead us straight to our apartment.

But when we got into the car, it was a diesel. It took a minute to adjust to the difference, in which time the mission president had already disappeared around a corner. Besides that, the car was out of gas. The mission president eventually found us at the gas station.

It was already dark outside, so we were terrified to drive, but we ventured out, following the president. On a busy freeway, we lost track of the mission president's car, and although we had a GPS, we'd never used one before. Then the lady in the GPS told us to take a wrong exit, and we got lost. Luckily, the mission president had given us a cell phone, so they called us and talked us through the directions. Unfortunately, we had never used a cell phone before either, and at first we couldn't figure out how to answer it! We laugh about that adventure now, but at the time, we were both pretty stressed.

Summary

- For some missions in the United States and Canada, you can drive your own car to your mission.
- The Missionary Travel Office will set up and purchase the flight to your mission. Check with them early if you have special seating preferences.
- It's helpful to have a family member or friend take you from the MTC to the airport.
- Get help moving all your heavy bags to your airline's check-in counter.
- Make sure you comply with TSA security requirements.[2]

- Bring cushions, food, and entertainment supplies for your long international flight, if you have one.
- Someone from your mission will meet you at the airport.

Notes

1. www.lds.org/callings/missionary/missionary-travel?lang=eng.
2. www.tsa.gov.

Chapter 11

THE MISSIONARY TRAINING CENTER

In order to make the transition from routine life to missionary life as smooth as possible, the Lord has provided almost all senior missionary couples with the opportunity to spend a week or two in the Missionary Training Center (MTC). You will be amazed at the impact this experience will have on your missionary life. It is truly inspired.

Let me give you one quick example, so you'll get a feel for what the MTC is all about.

For one of the MTC lessons, we were paired with another couple to do a missionary role-play. I immediately thought, "I can't role-play being a missionary. It will feel so fake." But we decided to give it our best effort.

For the activity, one couple was asked to be the missionaries, and the other couple was supposed to be the investigators. But the thing that made it work so well was that the teacher asked us (the ones role-playing as the investigators) to think of a family member or friend who was either not a member or who was inactive. We were to assume that person's character as we did the role-play. My husband and I decided to be a friend, who was gay, and her nonmember roommate. We figured we'd really give the other couple something difficult to deal with.

Well, they played the role of missionaries who came to visit us and assess our needs as children of God. The assignment was for them to first assess, and then to go off and counsel together on what could be done to bring gospel blessings into our lives. Then they were to come back and report what they thought would do that. After their assessment visit, that lovely missionary couple went aside and counseled together and prayed to know what would help us.

I still cry just thinking about their return "visit" to us. Their love for us was palatable and genuine, even in this "role-play" situation. Their suggestions on what to do for us were genuine and clearly inspired, and we knew that what they suggested probably would have worked and been a great benefit to our imaginary investigators. I was amazed; I realized that the Holy Ghost had actually participated in the role-play. The whole experience was incredible, and we felt humbled for ever questioning the validity of the MTC program.

Travel to the MTC

If you live close to the MTC, you will probably want to drive there. But if you live far away, the Church will pay for your flight. In order to have that flight scheduled, you will need to send in the postcard that is included in your missionary application.

The Church does not set up or pay for a shuttle from the airport to the MTC. You will need to schedule that online. They do, however, pay for a shuttle to take you from the MTC to the airport when you fly out to your mission.

Schedules

Your MTC time and training will vary, depending on your missionary assignment and duties. Generally, your first week in the MTC will be spent with a large group of other senior couples receiving general mission and gospel training. These sessions run from 8:00 a.m. to 4:30 p.m. every day, with an hour or so lunch break and shorter breaks between classes or presentations.

If you are assigned a second week at the MTC, that training will be related to your specific missionary duties and is done in small, individualized training groups. We were trained to be an office couple, so we were taught the computer skills and programs we would need to use to track missionaries, monitor car use, make purchases, record referrals, deal with apartments, create newsletters, and so on. But medical couples, employment couples, welfare couples, humanitarian couples, and many, many other kinds of missionaries are given specific instructions regarding their own assignments so that they will be prepared to do their work effectively as soon as they arrive in their missions.

So that's the overview. Now let's look at some MTC details you'll want to know.

Specifics

Before you leave for the MTC, you will receive an email from them asking where you plan to stay while you're at the MTC: you can live at home or at the MTC. Their email will provide information about housing, meals, and expenses. Your reply to their email will help them assign your housing and meals. Let them know of any special needs you have, and feel free to ask any questions.

If you are serving a mission in the US, you will be asked to bring your car or RV to your mission, and there will be a secure place for you to leave it during your stay at the MTC. However, if you are serving your mission in a foreign country, you will fly directly from the Salt Lake International Airport to your mission.

If you are lodging at the MTC, you will be assigned a room on either the main campus or in the west campus. If your classes are on the main campus and your housing on the west campus, a shuttle will be provided to and from your room. If your training is off the main campus, transportation will also be provided to and from your training.

Whether you choose to live at home and commute to the MTC or use MTC housing, you will use a card to record the meals eaten in the MTC cafeteria, and then you will pay a final bill before you leave for your mission. The cafeteria is divided into several buffet sections, so you can choose what you want to eat, and the food they serve is really good. In fact, it's so good and plentiful that many young missionaries gain ten pounds during their MTC stay.

Once your daily classes or training are over at 4:30, the rest of the day is in your hands. There are some evening devotionals and firesides you will probably want to attend, but you are free to plan your schedule as you choose. Wi-Fi is available in most of the MTC, so you can contact your family during your free time.

If you're staying one week, you will enter the MTC on Monday and leave on Friday. If you're staying two weeks, Saturday is preparation day, and you are free to leave the MTC and visit friends and family, shop, go to a movie, do your laundry, or just rest. You are also free to attend the temple during any of your free time. Missionaries are not charged for temple clothing rental. On Sunday, you can attend church at the MTC at your assigned time, or you can go to church with friends or family in the area.

Travel Documents

Sometime during your MTC visit, you will be given your travel documents, including your passport, with any necessary visa papers, and your one-way plane tickets. If you are nearing the end of your MTC stay and have not been contacted by the travel office branch there, don't hesitate to pay them a visit and see what the status of your travel documents is. They'll be able to access your account on their computers and see where your documents are.

Checking Out

Before you leave the MTC, you will be given a financial report that details what you owe for your stay. You can pay your account with cash, a credit or debit card, or a check. You will be charged a daily fee for housing and will be charged for every meal you ate in the cafeteria. You will not be charged for parking, Wi-Fi, linens, or transportation to and from classes or to the airport.

The MTC provides transportation to the Salt Lake International Airport, whether it is a shuttle or a ticket to take the commuter train. You can also have family or friends pick you up at the MTC and take you to the airport.

Summary

- The Church will pay for your flight to the MTC if you advise them ahead of time.

- You will need to set up and pay for a shuttle from the airport to the MTC.
- Your MTC stay will last one or two weeks.
- The first week involves general missionary training; the second week is specific to your assignment.
- You can choose to live at home if you live near the MTC.
- You will be charged for the meals you eat at the MTC and the housing if you lodge there.
- You will have free time in the evenings and on the weekends.
- You will be given your travel documents and tickets at the MTC.
- Transportation to and from your classes and to the airport will be provided.

Chapter 12

MISSION REALITIES

Before they arrive in the mission field, most senior couples have a preconceived idea of what their mission will be like. This idea has been formed over the years as they listen to homecoming talks in sacrament meeting and stories from returned missionaries. So when they get to the mission field, without actually realizing it, these faithful missionaries have set themselves up for a particularly disorienting surprise. Missions are real life, and missionary work is real work.

No missionary is going to tell his or her mother how challenging missionary life is. They love their mothers and want to protect them. Besides, who wants to discourage other people from serving missions? So missionaries tend to tell only the highlights of their missions, even in their weekly letters home. They talk about feeling close to the Spirit, of having their prayers answered, of finding golden investigators. What they don't mention is the discouragement, the physical exhaustion, the trials of faith, the crazy companions, and the emotional rollercoasters. Anyone who has served a mission knows the realities of mission life, but many first-time missionaries experience mission shock.

Expectations vs. Reality

Seniors who haven't served previous missions are particularly susceptible to mission shock. The realities of mission life can be dismaying. One of the first things they find out is that, unlike junior missionaries, they don't have a senior companion who already speaks the language, knows where to buy stuff, and knows how to work and when to relax. You and your wonderful companion are both greenies and are scrambling to figure out your new assignment, your new living arrangements, your new and unfamiliar environment, and, yes, even your new relationship.

At first, you may be quite surprised that you aren't having spiritual experiences every day, or even every week. You may think you are wasting too much time and may feel guilty when you take a nap, read a novel, or watch a video. You may drive your poor spouse mad fussing about not reading the scriptures enough, not exercising enough, not fasting enough, not being a *missionary*! You may even be positive that they are being a slacker and try to fix them.

Keep in mind Elder David B. Haight's insight: "Couples are not expected to work as many hours as the younger missionaries. Couples have many varied talents and are to prudently work to their strength and abilities. They are not expected to do more than they are able. Most couples have some limitations based on age and health. If they need to rest occasionally, they may do so."[1]

Relax. You *are* a missionary. Missions go on for a long time. This experience is not a sprint. It's a marathon. You will figure out a flow and a balance that both you and your spouse can live with, and you *will* have spiritual experiences—just not on demand.

You will learn more about yourself and the gospel than you ever dreamed possible. But it will come drop by drop by drop, and it will be much more difficult if you get angry, depressed, critical, or impatient. Just go serve. Don't sweat the small stuff. Don't worry; be happy—and all those other clichés you've heard, but didn't know applied to missionaries.

Balance

"To everything there is a season" (Ecclesiastes 3:1). On a mission, there is a time to work and a time to rest. There is a time to serve others and a time to serve yourself. There is a time to laugh and a time to cry. There is a time to love and a time to be loved. And all of those elements are what makes a mission such a memorable experience.

If you demand that your mission fit a certain preconceived pattern, you will deprive yourself of many glorious experiences. You will also make your spouse miserable, and you will have to repent of a lot of dumb mistakes.

Listen to the Spirit instead of listening to your anxieties. Work very hard at having a good time and making good memories.

One sister tells her regrets: "I wish I'd been happier on my mission. I just let the challenges and insecurities become my focus. Luckily, when I got home, I mostly forgot about all those picky things that bothered me and remembered the joy and satisfaction I got from learning to love the people I worked with."

Although there are many, many different mission assignments, let's look at two of the most common mission experiences.

Office Missions

Some types of missions are much less flexible and more mundane than you would imagine. In a mission office, you have more defined tasks, and you often work separately from your spouse. The same is true for area office missions, visitors' center missions, historical sites missions, and many other specialty missions. In a mission or area office, it actually doesn't feel very spiritual spending day after day filing papers, sending out letters, redoing the transfer board, or recording expenses. You may think, "How is this spreading the gospel?" But realistically, spending day after day tramping the streets and knocking on doors doesn't feel very spiritual either. Most of the time, missions are not all that exciting.

However, if you take the time to pray about your mission assignment, you will begin to understand how you are personally helping to gather Heavenly Father's chosen children. Someone needs to support the mission president and the junior missionaries as they scramble to find listening ears. Someone needs to keep life in order. Someone needs to make sure the cars run and the apartments are not full of roaches.

One senior office couple visited a missionary apartment, only to find that the missionaries had no functioning light fixtures. Instead of getting the problem fixed, the missionaries had simply strung Christmas lights all around the rooms. If missionaries don't have senior couples checking on them, they often forget to pick up their clothes, wash the dishes, clean the shower, or wash their sheets. Sometimes they don't even use sheets, and sometimes they lose their sheets! You are the parent they left at home. You can love them, encourage them, and feed them. You can answer their doctrinal questions and help them overcome temptations. You can help them have hope.

You are worth your weight in gold—and that's a lot of gold for most of us.

Senior office couples make mission presidents' lives possible, and consequently, mission presidents all over the world are begging for more and more couples.

MLS (Member and Leader Support) Missions

Unlike junior missions or office missions, MLS (and also some humanitarian, public affairs, medical, and CES) missions are more "choose your own adventure" experiences. There isn't a set schedule for you. There isn't a set task for you to do. There isn't even a set of expectations. You and your spouse get to make your own mission.

Although this flexibility seems daunting at first and may scare you to death, it is actually a really, really fun opportunity. You get to look at your personal talents and life experiences and decide how you can best bless the lives of those you have been assigned to serve.

Some senior MLS missionaries give haircuts. Some teach piano lessons. Some teach dance lessons. Some teach English or literacy lessons. Some make cookies. Some teach sewing skills. You and your spouse can analyze the needs of the area you serve in, evaluate what you have to offer, recognize your personal limitations and health restrictions, and then go to the Lord with some ideas.

Some of your plans will work out very well. Some will be complete disasters. What sounded good on paper may be a total waste of time. But, boy, will you learn a lot. And as you wander around a village or climb a steep, muddy path searching for lost members, you will see the people and the Church and your spouse in ways you never would have as a tourist or a stay-at-home member.

You'll go to support a weak branch, thinking you will teach them how the Church works and how to teach a class and how to run a meeting, but you'll discover that they are teaching you more than you could ever teach them. They'll teach you how to listen, how to be humble, how to learn, how to be patient in affliction, how to rely on God, and how to love. You will never be the same person again. Ever. And you thought you were going to help *them*.

No, your mission will not be what you expected, but it will be so much more than you ever realized it could be.

Summary

- You and your spouse will both be greenies. You have no senior, experienced companion.
- You will have spiritual experiences—just not on demand.
- Missions need a balance between work and rest.
- Office missions support missionaries and mission presidents.
- Member and Leader Support (MLS) missions support wards and branches.
- MLS missions are a "choose your own adventure" experience.
- Your mission will be better than you ever expected.

Notes

1. David B. Haight, "Couple Missionaries—'A Wonderful Resource,'" *Ensign*, February 1996.

Chapter 13

CULTURE SHOCK

People eat *fish eyes* here?" "What is that awful smell?" "Everyone talks so *loud*." You think you're pretty open-minded and world-wise when you leave for your mission. You've read about your new country. You've seen photos and watched videos. You think you know what to expect. But you don't. Experiencing the reality of life in a different culture, whether that culture is in the southern US, New York City, Uganda, or Taiwan, you're going to learn to see life with new and better eyes. Let's look at some common cultural surprises.

Traffic

One of the first things you'll notice, maybe even as you travel to the mission home from the airport, is the traffic. Different countries have different traffic laws and expectations. In some countries, obeying traffic laws is an option, not a requirement. Left turn lanes are not lanes; they are groups of cars that can turn left whenever they feel like it. Passengers put their hands out the window and wave to claim right-of-way. Driving is an adventure indeed. Members and other missionaries will help you figure out local traffic customs, and after a very short time, you too will drive like a native, though perhaps a bit more cautiously. You will begin to have a sense of what is appropriate and what isn't, what is safe and what isn't.

Many countries use only small, gas-efficient cars. Most don't have pickup trucks at all. Lots of countries have numerous scooters and bicycles because the roads are very narrow and cars are too expensive to buy and maintain. Initially, the whine of scooters and the blare of horns will make you crazy, but before long, you won't even notice them. You may even honk your own horn once or twice, just to feel culturally assimilated.

Smells

When you first arrive in a new country, you will notice that it smells different than you're used to. Some countries have open sewers. Sometimes the smells come from garbage piles. Some odd smells come from spices you're not used to. Some smells come from people who don't bathe as often as they do in the US or who eat lots and lots of garlic and onions.

In some countries, people sweep the gutters daily and keep the sidewalk spotless. In others, it is perfectly acceptable to throw trash out bus windows, and garbage may be collected once a month or not at all. As a result, countries are going to smell differently. But in almost no time at all, your nose will become so accustomed to the smells in your new country that you won't notice them.

I once asked a Brazilian sister who had visited the United States what she noticed was different in the US. She said the whole country smelled like hot grease—from all the fast-food restaurants. So I guess everyone thinks a new country smells odd.

Food

It's amazing how much food matters to our comfort level. When we can't eat what we like or when we are expected to eat food we don't like, we start to feel anxious. Other cultures eat animals or parts of animals that we have never even *considered* eating. When you're invited to dinner at a member's or investigator's home and they serve something you don't recognize, or worse, something you do recognize, you'll wonder if you can force yourself to eat it. Never fear. Local food is often safer and healthier than most of the processed, salt-, sugar-, and chemical-laden food you eat every day in the US.

Besides, as a senior couple, you cook almost all your own meals. You may not be able to find some ingredients you normally use, and some local ingredients will function differently in your recipes, but in no time at all, you will be making fabulous home-cooked meals.

Grocery stores in other countries are one of my favorite cultural experiences. Right next to the wrapped pork chops, you may find wrapped pig's ears. In Portugal, whenever we entered a grocery store, we were blasted with a strong fish smell. That's because almost every grocery store in Portugal has at least a twenty-foot-long tray of fresh fish, laid out on ice. They also have entire aisles dedicated solely to olive oil, in all its amazing varieties. In South Africa, they had aisles dedicated to white cornmeal, which locals used to make a popular dish called *pap*, and aisles for fermented milk, which is somewhat like yogurt. The number and variety of unusual fruits and vegetables in a new country is always fun to investigate and experiment with too.

In addition, because you are so accustomed to eating processed food that has been augmented with flavor enhancers and other chemicals, the natural food in other countries will initially taste very bland. But that natural food is so much better for you, as long as you wash it carefully and cook it thoroughly.

Local members may be just as shocked that you don't eat cow intestines or fish heads as you are shocked that they do. But they'll also be surprised that your cookies are so extremely sweet and that you add salt to your cakes. Your culture is as strange to them as theirs is to you.

By the time your mission is finished, you will have found local foods that you absolutely love and will really miss when you go home.

Apartments

Your apartment will initially be part of your culture shock. You may be surprised to find that your oven has only three settings: high, medium, and low. Or that you have no oven at all. You may be unhappy to find that you have no central heat or air conditioning. You may find it difficult to use only bottled water, even when you brush your teeth. You may even be dismayed to find that each room has one light, a single low-wattage bulb hanging from a long cord. Your fridge may be small, and your hot water may be inadequate.

You will find that light switches are in unaccustomed places, faucets function in new and unusual ways, and toilets flush with chains or knobs instead of handles. Everything still works. You just have to get used to new interaction patterns. Mostly, you will find that your apartment seems small and old, and you probably won't be used to having another family living just on the other side of your wall.

Realistically, though, you won't be in your apartment all day. You'll be out doing missionary work. And honestly, since your kids and grandkids won't be visiting all the time, you don't really need a huge family room and ten boxes of toys.

Personal Space

Cultures often view personal space differently. In some countries, people stand very close to you when you're conversing, which may make you feel uncomfortable. In some countries, they even touch you. In other countries, they stand further away than you're used to or don't look you in the eye, making you think they are hiding something. Your automatic interpretation of their actions is probably inaccurate and misleading, so don't jump to conclusions.

In some cultures, people talk very loudly. You can clearly hear them talking in apartments near yours or across the street. Other cultures think it is Americans who are very loud and pushy.

Some cultures greet with hugs and/or kisses. When I was in Brazil, we greeted single sisters with a hug and a kiss on each cheek and married sisters with a hug and only one kiss. Trying to figure it all out, I once greeted a member of the bishopric with a kiss on the cheek by mistake! (However, the kissing protocols in Brazil may be different there now.)

In Portugal, where they also greet with kisses, one of the sisters showed me her perception of an American greeting. She stood quite far from me, stiffened up straight, and firmly put her hand out to shake mine. It was almost comical how unfriendly the greeting was from her point of view.

A Brazilian woman once told me she felt very nervous walking down empty residential streets in the US. In Brazil, people sit out on their front steps chatting and hang out their windows greeting people. She really missed the friendliness.

Communication

When you get your mission call, you may be determined to learn the language of your new country. The MTC even offers tutoring in languages. However, many very capable senior missionaries have discovered that senior brains have trouble retaining new grammar and vocabulary. The little you do retain isn't nearly enough to actually communicate with people well or understand them.

As a result, senior sisters, who are by nature relationship-oriented, may initially feel isolated and unhappy. They go to meetings and understand nothing. They try to help someone and can't express their feelings. They can't even give talks or say prayers in sacrament meeting.

But having language limitations is not as prohibitive as it seems at first. Many, many senior missionaries learn to communicate soul to soul. The people you serve will understand you perfectly well. They'll know that you care about them. They'll also know if you are feeling critical and negative toward them. A smile, a hug, and a kiss say so much more than what you wanted to say with words. Unawares, the gift of tongues seems to make things work out.

You can also have your spouse, or someone else who speaks both English and the local language, translate your basic testimony, the simple prayer you want to say, or your talk. Then you can memorize or read just that short translated piece. The members will love you for your efforts.

Frequently, people around the world have studied English and speak it fairly well. Members often understood when we said a word in English that we couldn't remember in Portuguese. But beware. People also understand things you say

123

in English that you don't intend them to. Only say kind and positive things in any language.

Possessions

One senior sister who had served a mission in Fiji said that in that country your possessions were considered communal property, more or less. People thought it was perfectly natural to enter her apartment and take something they needed.

In other countries, thievery is the norm. Using a cell phone when you are walking down the street is an invitation to have it taken. And if you have something sitting on the seat of your car, you're to blame if someone breaks the window and takes it.

Your mission office will orient you on the expectations of your local culture and what you should do to protect your possessions.

Schedules

Some cultures are very time-oriented. Meetings start and end on time and follow agendas. Appointments are kept. People expect you to be prompt and organized. In other cultures, however, time is relative. Meetings start when most people finally get there, and the meetings may go well over the time allotted. In these cultures, people are more valued than schedules, so talking to someone in the hall is more important than getting to class on time.

When I once tried to get a ward activity started that was already an hour late, a member chastised me for being too concerned about unimportant details. After all, we were just there to enjoy each other's company. Who cared if the activity actually started on time?

Gender Dominance

In many countries throughout the world, men are still dominant. Sometimes women and children walk behind the men and eat separately or after the men. In some countries, you will find that the sisters in the Church don't make comments in classes that include men. They're still hesitant in Relief Society, but they feel much less inhibited when only sisters are present.

As Americans, we can't even imagine living with the amount of gender discrimination that exists in other countries. But we can be patient and courteous, respecting cultural differences, even if we don't accept them. Change takes time, and forcing your cultural expectations on others can actually be counterproductive.

Laws

America is a country that values and respects the rule of law—except maybe speed limits. We expect the police and government officials to follow the law, and if they don't, we chastise them publicly. We expect contractors to build according to legal specifications. We expect food to be safe to eat. And people who break the law are punished.

In some countries, laws are guidelines or ideals, not mandates. In those countries, no one really expects the police to be honest or the buildings to be built to code. Bribes and corruption are the norm and are viewed as an efficient and appropriate way to conduct business. However, Church policy is strictly against participating in this mode of doing business.

When you first get to a mission in this kind of country, you may be appalled and frustrated at the lack of adherence to laws. You may feel threatened and unsafe. But with the help of your mission president, you will learn how to handle the new system and function in it without conflict. Do check with your mission president on the best way to handle corruption at any level. Don't let the lack of respect for laws distress you or make you anxious. Pray for guidance, and be wise as you serve.

Conclusion

Yes, cultural shock can be, well, shocking. When you begin your mission, everything will seem different and everything will feel uncomfortable. But in a short time, you will be able to relax and enjoy the differences—perhaps even savor them. In Portugal, we smiled when the street we were on was too narrow to turn left. The solution? They had simply cut away part of the building on the corner so a car could squeeze by.

You will discover that new experiences and adventures make you appreciate your own culture and other cultures more. In fact, when I returned from Brazil, I even brought a Brazilian cookbook home so I could duplicate some of the wonderful food I had there. Much to my chagrin, however, even when I followed the recipes exactly, they didn't turn out right. American ingredients just weren't the same as Brazilian ones. Reverse culture shock! Who would have thought?

Summary

- Initially, cultural differences in your new country may make you uncomfortable.
- Traffic laws and expectations vary from culture to culture.
- Every country has its own unique smell—some pleasant, and some not so pleasant.
- The food in other countries is often healthier than food in the United States.

- Your apartment will be smaller and will function differently than you are used to.
- Personal space expectations differ from country to country. Many countries greet with kisses on the cheek.
- Since learning a new language is fairly difficult for most seniors, you will become adept at communicating soul to soul.
- In many countries, possessions are free to take if you leave them unattended.
- Countries vary dramatically on how prompt you and others are expected to be.
- Many women throughout the world are still dominated by men. Be patient and courteous as you work with both genders.
- In some countries, laws are guidelines or ideals, not mandates.
- Culture shock can be difficult to deal with, but it is temporary. Before you know it, you'll be functioning in the new culture quite comfortably.

Chapter 14

MARRIAGE ADJUSTMENTS

In earlier chapters, I mentioned that your marriage experiences on a mission may be different than your marriage at home. The extent of those differences may actually surprise you. In fact, figuring out how to agree on time management, household duties, missionary planning, apartment organization and maintenance, money management, and many, many other issues can be challenging.

For most of your marriage, you and your spouse have functioned in separate spheres. You had your job, and they had theirs, whether it was working at home or away from home. Most of the time, you had your church calling, and they had theirs. In fact, you likely had to schedule a date in order to have any time together at all.

Now, you're together all day every day, even if you're in an office setting where you're working on different tasks. Sister Robyn Levesque, who served with her husband in the Oregon Salem Mission, confessed, "The hardest part for us . . . was learning how to work together." She and her husband had been married for forty-two years. Yet she concluded, "This is the best thing we have ever done together."[1]

To put it bluntly, while serving a mission together, you can get on each other's nerves. I remember the first time my husband and I went grocery shopping together in Portugal, I finally had to tell him to go shop on a different aisle. He was scrutinizing every single item I had decided to put in the cart, debating whether we really, really needed that and whether the price was actually the very best possible deal. I thought I'd go crazy. In fact, we had no idea that we had such different shopping styles because we had rarely shopped together at home. When we returned to our apartment, thoroughly frustrated, we sat down and talked about the experience and how to handle shopping more effectively.

Sister Sheri McMurtrey was serving in the England London South Mission with her husband, Gary, when she advised, "Learn how to resolve disagreements. . . . Learn to build each other up." She added, "Communication is a key and something we are still trying to do better at. I am also still learning to be tolerant of our differences, which is difficult for me as I assume something means one thing and am not always right."[2]

Because your spouse may have been on a mission previously, because he or she may speak the local language better than you, and because one of you may have had a secretary in your previous job, without thinking, you may assume that one of you is the senior companion and that your spouse is to function as your assistant. Or since you have spent years managing your job, whether it is in the home or out, without thinking, you may assume you are an expert at how life should generally function. You want to decide how things should be organized, when and what you should eat, what is necessary for you to be spiritual, and how to interact with your family. So it's not surprising that your two worlds will collide as you try to create one productive, compatible, and, yes, even happy missionary experience.

Here are a few ideas that may help you manage your missionary marriage:

1. Schedule time to communicate. Don't just assume that it'll happen automatically. Junior missionaries have companionship planning (as explained in *Preach My Gospel*), and so should you. But don't just plan your day. Talk about problems you're having, things that frustrate you, and personal trials you are dealing with. Also talk about the really amazing things you are learning, the wonderful people you are working with, and the spiritual growth you are experiencing. Make your mission a joint mission by talking about it.

2. Study the scriptures and the gospel together. You may or may not have scheduled scripture study with your spouse when you were at home. But on your mission, it's important to have a daily time to share the gospel with each other, to discuss the scriptures together, and to build your testimonies. This should be a shared experience, not one spouse lecturing the other about gospel doctrine. Talk about how you want to approach your gospel study. Do you want to study a topic? Do you want to read and discuss a chapter? Do you want to take turns presenting an idea? Your gospel study time will become a treasured part of your missionary day if you plan properly.

3. Go on a date every single week. That's part of what preparation day is supposed to be for. If you spend the whole day doing laundry, shopping, cleaning, and reading books, you'll miss out on essential nourishment for your marriage. Missions don't need to

be spiritual and focused all the time. You can actually take time to have fun together.

4. If it's not safe to go out at night in your mission, have a date during the day. As senior missionaries, you are allowed to go to movies, go to dances, swim, visit historical sites, travel to nearby cities within your mission, go out to eat, go to parks and recreational sites, visit museums, and experience many more adventures. Surf the Internet to see what fun activities are available in your area and plan a month's worth of dates during one of your daily planning councils.

5. Talk about expectations and chores. Since you're both working all day, who should fix dinner when you both get home exhausted? Who does the dishes? Who cleans the apartment, and who takes the garbage to the dumpster down the street? Where do you want to keep the laundry? Where do you want to study? How are you going to handle the TV and other noise?

6. Remember, this is a *joint* discussion. You don't get to have your way all the time, but neither do you have to give in all the time. It's always such a shock to discover you actually may be wrong once or twice.

7. Don't belittle or criticize your companion or have arguments in public. In fact, it's lots better if you don't criticize or argue at all. If you find yourself disagreeing with something your spouse is doing, wait until your couple council to discuss it. Pray for guidance, understanding, and humility. Few things will destroy your effectiveness as missionaries like contention will. Your members and investigators will be embarrassed for you, and you will be embarrassed when you look back on your behavior.

8. Agree to disagree sometimes. You don't need to force your opinions on your spouse. If one of you wants to watch a soccer game on TV to relax and the other wants to read the scriptures, you can just do different things. In order to be able to read my novel while my husband watched a movie in our small apartment, I would take a folding camp chair into another room, even the bathroom if necessary, and shut the door. His accommodation was to turn the volume on the movie very low.

9. It is okay for couples to be apart sometimes. While junior missionaries must always be in each other's sight, senior missionaries have much more flexibility. One of you can go to a bishopric meeting without the other. One of you can go shopping with the members without the other. Don't make separateness your mission motif, by any means, but don't feel like you must be attached at the hip, either. Each of you needs personal space and time. Make sure to plan for it.

10. If you didn't study the Church's Marriage and Family Relations course before your mission (see chapter 3), study it together now. You can access the manual online at www.lds.org/manual/marriage-and-family -relations-instructors-manual?lang=eng.

You'll probably think of lots of other good ideas for keeping your mission marriage happy and nourished. Your marriage is more important than any other single aspect of your mission— more important than your schedule, your goals, your opinions, or your investigators. The new and improved marriage you develop on your mission will bless you and your family for the rest of your life and for eternity.

Summary

- Being together all day, every day can put stress on a marriage.
- You are a partnership—neither companion should dominate.
- Schedule time to communicate.
- Study the scriptures together daily.
- Go on dates every week.
- Discuss how to manage household chores fairly, since you are both working outside the apartment.
- Don't criticize or argue, especially in public.
- Agree to disagree on some issues.
- It's okay to be apart sometimes, but this is the exception, not the rule.
- Study the Church's Marriage and Family Relations course.

Notes

1. Robyn Levesque in "Senior Missionaries Answer Call to Serve," *Newsroom*, February 20, 2015, www.mormonnewsroom.org/article /senior-missionaries-answer-call-to-serve.
2. Sheri McMurtrey in Sunny Morton, "8 Tips for Preparing for a Senior Couples Mission," *LDS Living*, www.ldsliving.com/How -to-Prepare-for-a-Senior-Couples-Mission/s/74864.

Chapter 15

FAMILY CONCERNS

When senior couples are considering a mission, one of their greatest concerns is their family. If someone's not in a crisis at a given moment, they will be in the next while. And if you're a senior, you often have aging parents that you're concerned about. If you go on a mission, you'll miss births and baptisms and ordinations. You may even miss marriages and funerals. How can you possibly be away from everyone for so long?

Because this concern is so deeply felt and so widely experienced, the general authorities and other members have mentioned it frequently in their pleas for senior couples. Let's look at their advice.

For Perspective on Your Call

To an earlier generation of missionaries called to leave their families, the Lord offered this reassurance: "And if they will do this in all lowliness of heart, . . . I, the Lord, give unto them a promise that I will provide for their families."[1]

No senior missionary finds it convenient to leave. Neither did Joseph or Brigham or John or Wilford. They had children and grandchildren too. They loved their families not one whit less, but they also loved the Lord and wanted to serve Him. Someday we may meet these stalwarts who helped to establish this dispensation. Then will we rejoice that we did not seek the shadows when a call to missionary service came from the prophet, even in the autumn years of our lives.[2]

What greater gift could grandparents give their posterity than to say by deed as well as word, "In this family we serve missions!"[3]

On Missing Your Family

Some couples say, "I can't leave my grandchildren." My answer to them is: Your grandchildren will be there when you return, only they'll be two years older and even cuter than when you left them. Besides, what better legacy could you leave your grandchildren than the example of putting your testimony in action by serving a mission?[4]

As we consider couple missionary service, it is appropriate to involve our families in the same way. In family council meetings, we can give our children the opportunity to express their support, offer special assistance we may need, and receive priesthood blessings to sustain them in our absence. Where appropriate, we may be able to receive priesthood blessings from them as well.[5]

Sister Frandsen: "I worried about being away from children and grandchildren. However, there are amazing technological advances in communication available to senior missionaries. In some respects, I hear from and see more of our family than we ever did when we were home. We will have at least four grandchildren born while we are here, which we count as one of the greatest blessings of all.

Although I will miss holding the newborn babies, we will get to see pictures and videos as soon as each event happens. Rather than taking us away from family, in many ways our mission has brought us closer together."[6]

A faithful sister wrote: "The decision to serve a mission was not hard. But my ninety-year-old mother was extremely apprehensive about our leaving. She took great comfort when she heard that our families would be blessed as we serve." A faithful brother expressed similar concerns about leaving his elderly parents, to which his father responded: "Don't use your mother and me as an excuse not to go on a mission with your wife. You pray about it and follow the guidance of the Spirit."[7]

From Your Children's Point of View

Good people replaced our parenting functions better than we. . . . If a family problem has not yielded to prayer and fasting, a mission might be considered.[8]

My parents' letters taught volumes of gospel lessons. Stories of serving in an inner-city branch in Washington, DC; hiking to the bottom of the Grand Canyon to teach investigators; laboring with impoverished single mothers, wealthy stockbrokers, fishermen, potters, farmers, addicts, alcoholics, ministers, police officers, and the elderly—what better way to teach grandchildren the worth of every soul?

The greatest thing my parents have done for their posterity is to leave them in the Lord's hands and accept calls to serve Him as missionaries.[9]

Raymond and Gwen Petersen of Wyoming, USA, have served four missions. Their leaving on their second mission—to Samoa for the second time—was initially a challenge for their children, who didn't understand why their parents needed to serve *another* mission.

The family quickly realized what great blessings came from their service. "They had all prospered!" says Sister Petersen. "One couple who had been unable to have children were blessed with a baby boy, another had a miraculous healing from cancer, another with a struggling child saw great progress, and others had their best year in business."

Their hard work has left a trail of faith through their family line. "We have four grandsons on missions right now who tell us we were their inspiration to go," says Sister Petersen. "What could be more rewarding than that?"[10]

One Comforting Note

In cases of emergency or important family needs, senior missionaries can request a leave of absence to return, usually for up to ten days. This leave must be approved by your mission president, and you will be expected to pay for your flights home and back to your mission.

Be aware, though, that your leave should be for serious family needs. One couple I knew requested that they be given leave to attend a family reunion at Disney World, and their request was denied. Treat this privilege with respect.

The Church allows family members to visit you while you're on your mission. With your mission president's permission, you can even take some time off to show them around your mission and introduce them to your investigators.

In Conclusion

Apostles have promised senior couples that because of their mission service their posterity would be blessed for generations. They will miss you, and you will miss them. When they suffer, you will fast and pray for them. But you will also be amazed how they are blessed in your absence.

Family members will band together and support each other in ways you would never have anticipated. Children who have relied on your strength will develop their own faith and testimonies. Your whole family will find growth they didn't imagine was possible.

Elder Jeffrey R. Holland said, "Our message to all of our mature couples is simple: we dearly need you. We are doing everything we can to make it as convenient as possible for you to go. . . . The times cry out for it. There are people who need you. Please—go."[11]

Summary

- Early Church missionaries had to leave their loved ones. We can, too.
- Your families will be blessed while you serve.
- While you are gone, your children will support each other in ways that will strengthen your family for many years.
- You will set an example of missionary service to those in your family and others around you.
- Your posterity will be blessed for generations because of your service.
- You can get permission for a special leave of absence for important family needs.
- Your family members can visit you while you're on your mission.

Notes

1. Robert D. Hales, "Couple Missionaries: Blessings from Sacrifice and Service," *Ensign*, May 2005.

2. Russell M. Nelson, "Senior Missionaries and the Gospel," *Ensign*, November 2004.

3. Jeffrey R. Holland, "We Are All Enlisted," *Ensign*, November 2011.

4. David B. Haight, "Couple Missionaries—'A Wonderful Resource,'" *Ensign*, February 1996.

5. Hales, "Couple Missionaries: Blessings from Sacrifice and Service."

6. Kent D Watson, "Our Senior Missionaries," *Ensign*, September 2010.

7. Hales, "Couple Missionaries: Blessings from Sacrifice and Service."

8. Letter addressed to Elder Dallin H. Oaks from Dr. Brent and Carol Petersen, dated June 27, 2004. As cited in Russell M. Nelson, "Senior Missionaries and the Gospel," *Ensign*, November 2004.

9. Mark Crane, "Mission Blessings in the Golden Years," *Ensign*, December 2005.

10. Kendra Crandall Williamson, "Senior Missionaries: Responding to the Prophet's Call," *Ensign*, September 2012; italics in original.

11. Jeffrey R. Holland, *Deseret News*, September 14, 2011. As cited in Richard M. Romney, "Senior Missionaries: Needed, Blessed, and Loved," *Ensign*, April 2016.

Chapter 16

PRECIOUS MEMORIES

Every missionary couple will return from their mission with stories to tell of faith, love, and growth. Years after their mission, they will still cry thinking of the people they worked with and the joy they felt as they served. Here are some of my favorite memories.

Playing the Piano

When I arrived in Portugal, I was overwhelmed. I couldn't understand the Portuguese accent they spoke with, I was trying desperately to learn the computer programs the office used, and I was cold. It was winter, and there was no heat in Portuguese apartments. The first Sunday we were there, the mission president and his wife invited us to go with them to a district conference so we could see some of the beautiful countryside, and of course we said yes.

Right before the meeting began, President Walton asked me if I played the piano. Apparently no one at the conference played, even though the chapel had a piano. Well, I hadn't played the piano in forty years, but I had to admit that I played a little. They were thrilled to have any music at all, and they were willing to let me choose the two hymns for the meeting.

So I chose hymns I had learned fairly well many years ago. With lots of trepidation and a few errors, I played the hymns well enough for everyone to sing, and we were all glad for the music.

When we were transferred to the south of Portugal to serve as MLS missionaries, we found that a previous senior sister had taught two of the members in our branch to play a bit out of *Hymns Made Easy*, but they wanted me to take a turn playing too. Whenever one of them wasn't there for their turn, I was able to pinch hit. I got so I could actually fake the hymns fairly well and play them up to speed, skipping notes when necessary.

Then we attended another district conference, and the usual pianist didn't show up. The program was already printed, with "Praise to the Man" as the opening song, and they asked me to play at the last minute. "Praise to the Man" goes ninety miles an hour and has lots and lots of notes. But I managed to get at least the melody notes out fast enough, with an occasional bass chord so it would sound authentic. Weak as my playing was, I was willing to try, and the members seemed to think I was doing great. Somehow, my little offering was made into something wonderful. Whew!

A couple of months later, our branch begged me to teach piano lessons to two of the youth, and of course I said I would try. The Church has a simplified piano course available for missionaries, so we began with both of the kids (ten and thirteen years old) sitting at one piano, learning to find middle C. Unfortunately, almost immediately, I discovered that in Portugal they don't call the notes by the letters of the alphabet like I was used to. They call them *do, re, mi, fa, so, la, ti, do,* like in the movie *The Sound of Music.* So every time I mentioned a note, I'd have to sing the "Do, Re, Mi" song in my head to figure out what the note was called.

But the students did learn to play the piano and how to lead music. Thirteen-year-old Daniel was especially committed to learning, and he had a piano at home to practice on. Before long, both students were leading the music in meetings, and Daniel began to play the piano for priesthood meeting. I can't tell you how gratifying it was to see those teenagers grow and thrive as musicians. And Daniel continues to improve and play for the branch.

When we served our second mission in South Africa, a member of our ward knew how to play the piano very well, but when he didn't arrive on time, I would jump up and play whatever hymn had been announced for sacrament meeting. It was still scary, but I was better at faking the hymns than I had been in Portugal.

In Relief Society, however, I was the only pianist, and the sisters loved having piano music to sing to. One of my favorite memories is having the sisters sing quietly to the prelude music. And sometimes as I played postlude music, a group of sisters would gather around the piano and sing together way past the ending time for the meeting. I cried as I sang with them, and I still cry remembering the joy of the experience.

Finding the Mártires Family

As MLS missionaries in Southern Portugal, our tasks changed dramatically. Bruce was put in the branch presidency to help train the branch leadership. And we discovered that although over three hundred members were listed on the branch membership rolls, only about forty or fifty ever attended meetings. We were asked to find the missing members in the branch boundaries.

And so began one of our favorite mission experiences. What fun we had driving through the countryside, trying to find addresses. Of course, the GPS in our car was almost hopeless. But our Portuguese was much better after a year in the country.

We loved wandering through the medieval-age town of Faro looking for homes that turned out to be nonexistent. We even had a good time talking to strangers who now lived in the apartments our members had previously rented. And yes, we would invite them to learn about the Church, even though they would mostly say they weren't interested. Every once in a while, we would actually find an inactive member still living at the address in the branch list, and we would chat with them about the Church and invite them back.

Late one afternoon, we found the address of the Mártires family, who hadn't attended church for almost twenty years. We knocked on the door, and a woman leaned over the balcony above us, telling us that her husband was still at work. As we started to leave, Brother Mártires drove up and got out of his car. We introduced ourselves and asked him how he had been converted to the Church. Then we stood and listened for more than a half an hour as he bore testimony to us, telling about when two elders approached his house just as he was leaving for the hospital to see his baby daughter who was critically ill. The elders were invited to come along and subsequently, the baby was miraculously healed by a priesthood blessing.

Brother Mártires told us that he and his family now belonged to another church, but after remembering how he was converted he thought he might be interested in coming to one of our meetings again. We knew from the record that he had two inactive sons, so Bruce asked if we could come back another day and bring a video for him to invite his sons to watch. We were thrilled when he set an appointment for us to return.

When we arrived at the Mártires home, Brother Mártires and his sons were all dressed up in church clothes. However, these two sons were not the boys in our records, but were two other teenage sons we didn't know about, and they were not members of the Church. We showed *The First Vision* to them, bore our testimonies, and asked if the elders could come and teach them about the restored gospel. When Tiago, the oldest of the two boys, said yes, I nearly fainted for joy.

Not long after, both boys were baptized, and even though their father eventually stopped coming to church, the sons never missed a week. When Tiago gave his first sacrament meeting talk, he spoke of our initial meeting with them. He said he didn't remember almost anything of the video he watched, but he remembered the love he felt from us when we came to his home, and later he felt that same love from the members when he entered the chapel. The branch president took Tiago under his wing, and he later made Tiago his executive secretary. Oh, how we loved Tiago and Daniel.

Tiago was old enough to attend the youth center we had been asked to set up, so for the rest of our mission, Bruce taught institute lessons every week in Portuguese to Tiago and any other young adults who came, while I made American food for their dinner. Then we would play games and talk about their lives, school classes, and work.

Tiago spoke English very well, and he wanted to improve his English, so we often played our games using English.

Tiago was an expert strategist at UNO and beat us every time. Playing Scrabble in English, though, was almost impossible for him. How we laughed. How we loved each other. How we cried when our mission ended and we had to leave Tiago and Daniel, our own beloved boys.

When we began serving our second mission in Africa, we found out that Tiago had been called to serve a mission in Brazil, and Daniel was preparing for a mission as well.

Other Favorite Memories

- Praying to find parts for the broken, antique toilets in the missionary apartments—and finding them!
- In spite of my fears, singing a solo for a Christmas sacrament meeting, and then being asked to sing it again for the closing song.
- Walking through ancient ruins of palaces and forts, and strolling hand in hand along the beautiful Portuguese beaches.
- Hanging our clothes all over the apartment to dry because it was winter and we didn't have a clothes dryer.
- Eating citrus fruit straight from the orchard that surrounded our apartment.
- Speaking in sacrament meeting and having members yell out words I couldn't remember in Portuguese.
- Hearing the local soccer fans honking horns, singing, and dancing all night outside our apartment when their team won the national championship.
- Collecting stories of faith and courage from the African Saints to put on the website and publish in a book.

We Are as Ammon

Our mission in Africa was in the area office. Bruce did legal work and I worked on the area web page and the local section of the *Liahona*, the international version of the *Ensign*. We didn't have much contact with the local members, except at church on Sundays. However, we loved the work we did in the office.

One afternoon, I was reading the story of Ammon (one of my favorite superheroes), in Alma 17 of the Book of Mormon. As I read of him lifting his sword to defend the king's sheep, in my mind, I saw clearly my dear husband lifting his sword to defend the Saints in Africa. Only his sword was a sword of legal analysis and expertise. There were some poor decisions being promoted that could have threatened the Church's ability to function in the country, and like Ammon, he was using his talents to help the King protect and gather His sheep in Africa.

And then I realized that just as the youth in the Church sing, "we are as the army of Helaman."[1] I knew we, as senior missionaries, and in fact, we as members of God's Church everywhere, are as Ammon. We offer our talents to build the kingdom, and God magnifies them until they are swords of strength that gather and protect His sheep throughout the world. We are all, indeed, superheroes in God's hands as we offer to serve Him.

Conclusion

So whether you feel like a superhero right now or not, you too can be an instrument in God's hands to build up His kingdom, rescue His children, and strengthen His church. He doesn't care if you feel inadequate. All He asks for is a willing heart and a desire to serve. He'll send His Spirit to bless and inspire you. You'll find yourself being led, supported, and blessed as you prepare for your mission. It will just feel right.

Remember my account of our first senior mission call in the Introduction, when we weren't even retired yet? Let me tell you the rest of the story. We had never been wealthy, so preparing for retirement was a real concern for us. When the bishop asked us to consider quitting our jobs to go on a mission, we realized that retiring early would severely reduce our retirement benefits for the rest of our lives. And how would we pay the mortgage on our house? But we decided to take the leap of faith asked of us and submit our application.

Two weeks later, a friend called me, asking if I had stock in a company I had helped establish ten years before. I laughed. We had never owned stock of any kind. But she persisted. "Remember? They gave us stock for working for free that first year. Go look. Someone is buying stock in the company."

Miraculously, a week before, my husband had been searching through old files in the barn looking for a document, and he had noticed a file with a stock certificate in it. So when I asked him if he knew of any papers proving we owned stock, he knew exactly where to look. And we found we owned eleven thousand shares in the company!

Selling the stock gave us barely enough money to pay off our house. We applied for reduced retirement benefits, purchased all our missionary supplies from thrift stores, and had just enough money to pay our monthly mission costs.

But more important than the monetary blessings we received were the spiritual blessings that our family experienced. Our children saw God's hand work in our lives, and they bore testimony of it to their children, to their friends, and to their wards. They saw how our mission blessed us and how we were able to serve in spite of our weaknesses. They felt the Spirit as they read our weekly mission reports. They laughed with us and cried with us, and we all rejoiced together.

Now, your story will differ from mine, but it will be no less marvelous. Your mission will be tailored to your abilities and needs. Your family will be blessed in ways unique to them. And when you are done serving your mission, you will be filled with love for Heavenly Father and His children. In fact, you will give one of those amazing sacrament meeting homecoming talks that you always loved.

Before long, you will find yourself reading the Senior Missionary Opportunities Bulletin just to see what interesting mission experiences are available out there. And then you will think of far away Saints and begin to wonder if you should start planning for your next mission.

Notes

1. "We'll Bring the World His Truth (Army of Helaman)," *Children's Songbook*, 172–73.

Appendix A

USEFUL ONLINE RESOURCES

- Deseret Mutual Benefit Administrators (DMBA)
  www.dmba.com/ssmp
- Marriage and Family Relations Manual
  www.lds.org/manual/marriage-and-family-relations
  -instructors-manual
- Missionary Clothing Guidelines
  www.missionaryclothing.lds.org
- Missionary Handbook
  www.lds.org/manual/missionary-handbook
- Missionary Online Recommendation System
  www.lds.org/mss
- Missionary Travel
  www.lds.org/callings/missionary/missionary-travel
- Provo Missionary Training Center
  mtc.byu.edu/
- Senior Missionary Frequently Asked Questions
  beta.lds.org/bc/content/shared/content/english/pdf
  /missionary/senior-missionaries-faq-17-12-2000.pdf
- Senior Missionary Opportunities Bulletin
  www.lds.org/senioropportunities

- Senior Missionary Services
  Email the Senior Missionary Services at
  seniormissionaryservices@ldschurch.org
- Senior Missionary Stories
  www.lds.org/callings/missionary/senior
- US Transportation Security Administration
  www.tsa.gov
- Worldwide Electricity Standards and Plugs
  en.wikipedia.org/wiki/Mains_electricity_by_country
  and en.wikipedia.org/wiki/AC_power_plugs_and
  _sockets

Appendix B

WORLDWIDE VOLTAGE, FREQUENCY, AND PLUG TYPE

Country/State/Territory	Voltage (volts)	Frequency (hertz)	Plug Type
Abu Dhabi	230 V	50 Hz	G
Afghanistan	220 V	50 Hz	C/F
Albania	230 V	50 Hz	C/F
Algeria	230 V	50 Hz	C/F
American Samoa	120 V	60 Hz	A/B/F/I
Andorra	230 V	50 Hz	C/F
Angola	220 V	50 Hz	C
Anguilla	110 V	60 Hz	A/B
Antigua & Barbuda	230 V	60 Hz	A/B
Argentina	220 V	50 Hz	I
Armenia	230 V	50 Hz	C/F
Aruba	120 V	60 Hz	A/B/F
Australia	230 V	50 Hz	I
Austria	230 V	50 Hz	C/F
Azerbaijan	220 V	50 Hz	C/F
Azores	230 V	50 Hz	B/C/F
Bahamas	120 V	60 Hz	A/B
Bahrain	230 V	50 Hz	G

Country/State/ Territory	Voltage (volts)	Frequency (hertz)	Plug Type
Balearic Islands	230 V	50 Hz	C/F
Bangladesh	220 V	50 Hz	A/C/D/G/K
Barbados	115 V	50 Hz	A/B
Belarus	220 V	50 Hz	C/F
Belgium	230 V	50 Hz	C/E
Belize	110 V/220 V	60 Hz	A/B/G
Benin	220 V	50 Hz	C/E
Bermuda	120 V	60 Hz	A/B
Bhutan	230 V	50 Hz	C/D/G
Bolivia	230 V	50 Hz	A/C
Bonaire	127 V	50 Hz	A/C
Bosnia & Herzegovina	230 V	50 Hz	C/F
Botswana	230 V	50 Hz	D/G
Brazil	127 V/220 V	60 Hz	C/N
Brunei	240 V	50 Hz	G
Bulgaria	230 V	50 Hz	C/F
Burkina Faso	220 V	50 Hz	C/E
Burundi	220 V	50 Hz	C/E
Cambodia	230 V	50 Hz	A/C/G
Cameroon	220 V	50 Hz	C/E
Canada	120 V	60 Hz	A/B
Canary Islands	230 V	50 Hz	C/E/F
Cape Verde	230 V	50 Hz	C/F
Cayman Islands	120 V	60 Hz	A/B
Central African Republic	220 V	50 Hz	C/E
Chad	220 V	50 Hz	C/D/E/F
Channel Islands	230 V	50 Hz	C/G
Chile	220 V	50 Hz	C/L

Country/State/ Territory	Voltage (volts)	Frequency (hertz)	Plug Type
China	220 V	50 Hz	A/C/I
Christmas Island	230 V	50 Hz	I
Cocos (Keeling) Islands	230 V	50 Hz	I
Colombia	110 V	60 Hz	A/B
Comoros	220 V	50 Hz	C/E
Congo, Democratic Republic of the	220 V	50 Hz	C/D/E
Congo, Peoples Republic of	230 V	50 Hz	C/E
Cook Islands	240 V	50 Hz	I
Costa Rica	120 V	60 Hz	A/B
Ivory Coast	220 V	50 Hz	C/E
Croatia	230 V	50 Hz	C/F
Cuba	110 V/220 V	60 Hz	A/B/C/L
Curaçao	127 V	50 Hz	A/B
Cyprus	230 V	50 Hz	G
Czech Republic	230 V	50 Hz	C/E
Denmark	230 V	50 Hz	C/E/F/K
Djibouti	220 V	50 Hz	C/E
Dominica	230 V	50 Hz	D/G
Dominican Republic	120 V	60 Hz	A/B/C
Dubai	230 V	50 Hz	G
East Timor	220 V	50 Hz	C/E/F/I
Ecuador	120 V	60 Hz	A/B
Egypt	220 V	50 Hz	C/F
El Salvador	120 V	60 Hz	A/B
England	230 V	50 Hz	G
Equatorial Guinea	220 V	50 Hz	C/E

Country/State/ Territory	Voltage (volts)	Frequency (hertz)	Plug Type
Eritrea	230 V	50 Hz	C/L
Estonia	230 V	50 Hz	C/F
Ethiopia	220 V	50 Hz	C/F
Faeroe Islands	230 V	50 Hz	C/E/F/K
Falkland Islands	240 V	50 Hz	G
Fiji	240 V	50 Hz	I
Finland	230 V	50 Hz	C/F
France	230 V	50 Hz	C/E
French Guiana	220 V	50 Hz	C/D/E
Gabon	220 V	50 Hz	C
Gambia	230 V	50 Hz	G
Gaza Strip	230 V	50 Hz	C/H
Georgia	220 V	50 Hz	C/F
Germany	230 V	50 Hz	C/F
Ghana	230 V	50 Hz	D/G
Gibraltar	230 V	50 Hz	G
Great Britain	230 V	50 Hz	G
Greece	230 V	50 Hz	C/F
Greenland	230 V	50 Hz	C/E/F/K
Grenada	230 V	50 Hz	G
Guadeloupe	230 V	50 Hz	C/E
Guam	110 V	60 Hz	A/B
Guatemala	120 V	60 Hz	A/B
Guinea	220 V	50 Hz	C/F/K
Guinea-Bissau	220 V	50 Hz	C
Guyana	120 V/240 V	60 Hz	A/B/D/G
Haiti	110 V	60 Hz	A/B
Honduras	120 V	60 Hz	A/B
Hong Kong	220 V	50 Hz	G

Country/State/ Territory	Voltage (volts)	Frequency (hertz)	Plug Type
Hungary	230 V	50 Hz	C/F
Iceland	230 V	50 Hz	C/F
India	230 V	50 Hz	C/D/M
Indonesia	230 V	50 Hz	C/F
Iran	230 V	50 Hz	C/F
Iraq	230 V	50 Hz	C/D/G
Ireland	230 V	50 Hz	G
Ireland, Northern	230 V	50 Hz	G
Isle of Man	230 V	50 Hz	C/G
Israel	230 V	50 Hz	C/H
Italy	230 V	50 Hz	C/F/L
Jamaica	110 V	50 Hz	A/B
Japan	100 V	50 Hz/ 60 Hz	A/B
Jordan	230 V	50 Hz	C/D/F/G/J
Kazakhstan	220 V	50 Hz	C/F
Kenya	240 V	50 Hz	G
Kiribati	240 V	50 Hz	I
Kosovo	230 V	50 Hz	C
Kuwait	240 V	50 Hz	F
Kyrgyzstan	220 V	50 Hz	C/F
Laos	230 V	50 Hz	A/B/C/E/F
Latvia	230 V	50 Hz	C/F
Lebanon	230 V	50 Hz	C/D/G
Lesotho	220 V	50 Hz	M
Liberia	120 V	60 Hz	A/B
Libya	230 V	50 Hz	C/L
Liechtenstein	230 V	50 Hz	C/J
Lithuania	230 V	50 Hz	C/F

Country/State/ Territory	Voltage (volts)	Frequency (hertz)	Plug Type
Luxembourg	230 V	50 Hz	C/F
Macau	220 V	50 Hz	G
Macedonia, Republic of	230 V	50 Hz	C/F
Madagascar	220 V	50 Hz	C/E
Madeira	230 V	50 Hz	C/F
Malawi	230 V	50 Hz	G
Malaysia	240 V	50 Hz	G
Maldives	230 V	50 Hz	C/D/G/J/ K/L
Mali	220 V	50 Hz	C/E
Malta	230 V	50 Hz	G
Marshall Islands	120 V	60 Hz	A/B
Martinique	220 V	50 Hz	C/D/E
Mauritania	220 V	50 Hz	C
Mauritius	230 V	50 Hz	C/G
Mayotte	230 V	50 Hz	C/E
Mexico	127 V	60 Hz	A/B
Micronesia, Federated States of	120 V	60 Hz	A/B
Moldova	230 V	50 Hz	C/F
Monaco	230 V	50 Hz	C/E/F
Mongolia	230 V	50 Hz	C/E
Montenegro	230 V	50 Hz	C/F
Montserrat	230 V	60 Hz	A/B
Morocco	220 V	50 Hz	C/E
Mozambique	220 V	50 Hz	C/F/M
Myanmar	230 V	50 Hz	A/C/D/G/I
Namibia	220 V	50 Hz	D/M
Nauru	240 V	50 Hz	I

Country/State/Territory	Voltage (volts)	Frequency (hertz)	Plug Type
Nepal	230 V	50 Hz	C/D/M
Netherlands	230 V	50 Hz	C/F
New Caledonia	220 V	50 Hz	C/F
New Zealand	230 V	50 Hz	I
Nicaragua	120 V	60 Hz	A/B
Niger	220 V	50 Hz	C/D/E/F
Nigeria	230 V	50 Hz	D/G
Niue	230 V	50 Hz	I
Norfolk Island	230 V	50 Hz	I
North Korea	220 V	50 Hz	C
Norway	230 V	50 Hz	C/F
Oman	240 V	50 Hz	G
Pakistan	230 V	50 Hz	C/D
Palau	120 V	60 Hz	A/B
Palestine	230 V	50 Hz	C/H
Panama	120 V	60 Hz	A/B
Papua New Guinea	240 V	50 Hz	I
Paraguay	220 V	50 Hz	C
Peru	220 V	60 Hz	A/C
Philippines	220 V	60 Hz	A/B/C
Pitcairn Islands	230 V	50 Hz	I
Poland	230 V	50 Hz	C/E
Portugal	230 V	50 Hz	C/F
Puerto Rico	120 V	60 Hz	A/B
Qatar	240 V	50 Hz	G
Réunion	230 V	50 Hz	C/E
Romania	230 V	50 Hz	C/F
Russia	220 V	50 Hz	C/F
Rwanda	230 V	50 Hz	C/J

Country/State/ Territory	Voltage (volts)	Frequency (hertz)	Plug Type
Saba	110 V	60 Hz	A/B
Saint Barthélemy	230 V	60 Hz	C/E
Saint Helena	230 V	50 Hz	G
Saint Kitts & Nevis	230 V	60 Hz	D/G
Saint Lucia	230 V	50 Hz	G
Saint Martin	220 V	60 Hz	C/E
Saint Vincent & the Grenadines	110 V/230 V	50 Hz	A/B/G
Samoa	230 V	50 Hz	I
San Marino	230 V	50 Hz	C/F/L
São Tomé & Príncipe	230 V	50 Hz	C/F
Saudi Arabia	230 V	60 Hz	G
Scotland	230 V	50 Hz	G
Senegal	230 V	50 Hz	C/D/E/K
Serbia	230 V	50 Hz	C/F
Seychelles	240 V	50 Hz	G
Sierra Leone	230 V	50 Hz	D/G
Singapore	230 V	50 Hz	G
Sint Eustatius	110 V/220 V	60 Hz	A/B/C/F
Sint Maarten	110 V	60 Hz	A/B
Slovakia	230 V	50 Hz	C/E
Slovenia	230 V	50 Hz	C/F
Solomon Islands	230 V	50 Hz	G/I
Somalia	220 V	50 Hz	C
Somaliland	220 V	50 Hz	C
South Africa	230 V	50 Hz	C/D/M/N
South Korea	220 V	60 Hz	F
South Sudan	230 V	50 Hz	C/D
Spain	230 V	50 Hz	C/F

Country/State/ Territory	Voltage (volts)	Frequency (hertz)	Plug Type
Sri Lanka	230 V	50 Hz	D/G
Sudan	230 V	50 Hz	C/D
Suriname	127 V/230 V	60 Hz	A/B/C/F
Swaziland	230 V	50 Hz	M
Sweden	230 V	50 Hz	C/F
Switzerland	230 V	50 Hz	C/J
Syria	220 V	50 Hz	C/E/L
Tahiti	220 V	50 Hz/ 60 Hz	C/E
Taiwan	110 V	60 Hz	A/B
Tajikistan	220 V	50 Hz	C/F
Tanzania	230 V	50 Hz	D/G
Thailand	230 V	50 Hz	A/B/C/O
Togo	220 V	50 Hz	C
Tokelau	230 V	50 Hz	I
Tonga	240 V	50 Hz	I
Trinidad & Tobago	115 V	60 Hz	A/B
Tunisia	230 V	50 Hz	C/E
Turkey	230 V	50 Hz	C/F
Turkmenistan	220 V	50 Hz	C/F
Turks & Caicos Islands	120 V	60 Hz	A/B
Tuvalu	230 V	50 Hz	I
Uganda	240 V	50 Hz	G
Ukraine	230 V	50 Hz	C/F
United Arab Emirates	230 V	50 Hz	G
United Kingdom	230 V	50 Hz	G
United States of America	120 V	60 Hz	A/B

Country/State/ Territory	Voltage (volts)	Frequency (hertz)	Plug Type
Uruguay	220 V	50 Hz	C/F/L
Uzbekistan	220 V	50 Hz	C/F
Vanuatu	230 V	50 Hz	I
Vatican City	230 V	50 Hz	C/F/L
Venezuela	120 V	60 Hz	A/B
Vietnam	220 V	50 Hz	A/C/D
Virgin Islands (Britain)	110 V	60 Hz	A/B
Virgin Islands (USA)	110 V	60 Hz	A/B
Wales	230 V	50 Hz	G
Yemen	230 V	50 Hz	A/D/G
Zambia	230 V	50 Hz	C/D/G
Zimbabwe	240 V	50 Hz	D/G

Sources

1. "Plug, socket & voltage by country," *World Standards*, last modified May 16, 2016, accessed December 5, 2016, www .worldstandards.eu/electricity/plug-voltage-by-country/. See also, en.wikipedia.org/wiki/Mains_electricity_by_country and www .equitech.com/support/worldpwr.html.

Appendix C

PLUG/SOCKET TYPES

Type A

Type B

Type C

Type D

Type E

Type F

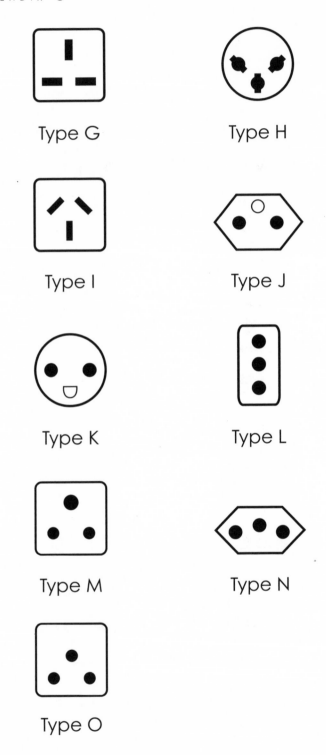

Type G

Type H

Type I

Type J

Type K

Type L

Type M

Type N

Type O

Sources

1. "Plug & socket types," *World Standards*, last modified April 30, 2016, accessed December 5, 2016, www.worldstandards .eu/electricity/plugs-and-sockets/. See also, www.interpower.com /cgi-bin/ic.cgi/guidelist.p, www.iec.ch/worldplugs, and en.wikipedia .org/wiki/AC_power_plugs_and_sockets.

Index

O

Office couples 28–29, 44, 108, 116
Online resources 43, 149

P

Packing 87, 91–99. *See also* Luggage
Passports 34, 39, 41–43, 45, 97, 99–100, 110
Permissions 34
Phones. *See* Calling home
  Cell phone 47, 81–82, 89
  Skype 20, 83
  Smartphone 82, 85–86, 89, 91
  VoIP 83–84, 89
Preach My Gospel 14–15, 21

S

Skills 19–20, 22, 25, 31, 108, 116

T

Taxes 50, 54
Temple recommend 43, 45
Tithing and offerings 49, 54
Traffic 118, 126
Travel 44, 97, 100, 107, 149
  Driving 100–101, 104, 109
    RV 100–101, 109
  Flying 93, 99, 101–3, 105, 110
  Missionary Travel Office 40–41, 44–45, 94, 101, 104
  Transportation Security Administration (TSA) 95, 102–4, 150

V

Visas 16, 39–43, 45, 50

W

Ward Mission Fund 48, 50

About the Author

Marnae Wilson loves an adventure, whether it's climbing inside a Mayan pyramid in Mexico or checking out the feasibility of study abroad programs in Mozambique, Africa. She has experienced the adventure of starting and running a private junior high—high adventure indeed. She's served LDS missions on three continents, two of them as a senior sister. But the greatest adventure of all was marrying her nonconformist best friend and raising seven very independent children.

Scan to visit

0 26575 20116 1

www.marnaewilson.com